The Complete Guide to

SALMON

The Complete Guide to

SALMON

A CULINARY COMPANION FOR AMERICA'S FAVORITE FISH

JAMES E. GRIFFIN

FOREWORD BY JOE GURRERA

New York Paris London Milan

This cookbook is dedicated to all of the hardworking men and women throughout the seafood supply chain—particularly those who operate behind the scenes or out on the ocean. Your hard work doesn't go unnoticed, nor is it unappreciated. Thank you for helping to feed a hungry planet.

CONTENTS

FOREWORD
BY JOE GURRERA

Years ago, a mutual friend introduced me to Jim Griffin, a chef, seafood expert, and a professor at Johnson & Wales, who was also a fan of shopping at Citarella, my gourmet markets. We hit it off instantly. In each other, we immediately recognized a passion for quality food and an enthusiasm for seafood, in particular, that became the foundation of our friendship.

I started out in the seafood business more than forty years ago and have grown multiple companies in New York City, including a wholesale seafood business, a purveying business for hospitality, and retail gourmet markets. While the city changes, some things stay the same—like our commitment to the absolute best-quality fish you can find in the country. When it comes to something as magnificent as seafood, it's important to never cut corners.

I've had the great privilege of working in a business I love, and getting to meet people like Jim, whose enthusiasm and quest for knowledge make him such a great colleague. Like me, Jim finds joy in sharing food with family and friends. Food is primal. So many important memories and gatherings are centered around food. To be a part of that is a powerful thing. Although we love it all, seafood is the foundation for both of us. Growing up in Gloucester, Massachusetts, gave Jim a lifelong affinity for fish—where to find them, how to cook them, and how to protect them for future generations.

I've worked closely with Jim over the years. He's not just a gifted chef; he's a dedicated educator and a consultant who truly understands ingredients from every angle—from sourcing to the plate. When he decided to write the definitive book on salmon, I knew it would be something special, built on a foundation of both culinary excellence and deep knowledge.

Salmon, as you know, is a cornerstone of what we do at Citarella. It's a magnificent fish, incredibly versatile and nourishing. But to truly appreciate it, you need to understand it. Jim gets that. He's put together a guide that covers all the essential ground, walking you through the different species, explaining the importance of sourcing and sustainability—topics critical to us at Citarella—and showing you how to handle and prepare salmon so you get the best possible result, every single time. This foundational knowledge, the kind we value so highly, is all here.

And then there are the recipes. As you'd expect from a chef of Jim's caliber, the culinary ideas in this book are outstanding. They are diverse, creative, and approachable, offering countless ways to transform beautiful salmon into unforgettable meals. Whether you're looking for a simple weeknight meal or something to truly impress, Jim provides the guidance you need.

This book is a valuable resource for anyone who loves salmon or wants to learn more about it. Chef Griffin has done a remarkable job combining essential information with inspiring recipes. Trust in the quality of the fish you start with—the kind you'll find if you shop with care—and trust in Jim's expertise to guide you the rest of the way. You're in excellent hands.

OPPOSITE: Jim Griffin holding a steelhead salmon and standing beside Joe Gurrera at the Fulton Fish Market, Bronx, New York, June 2025.

Part 1

AN INTRODUCTION TO SALMON

FROM LEFT TO RIGHT: steelhead salmon, Atlantic salmon, king salmon

INTRODUCTION

Salmon. The very word evokes images of powerful fish leaping against cascading currents, of silver scales catching the light, of rich, flavorful fillets gracing the finest tables. For many, salmon represents the pinnacle of seafood—globally available, versatile, nutritious, and undeniably delicious. Yet there is so much more to say about salmon and misinformation to correct. It is a fascinatingly complex fish with nuanced differences and a culinary potential that often goes unexplored. My own journey with this remarkable fish began, perhaps surprisingly, far from its native waters.

Growing up in Gloucester, Massachusetts, America's oldest seaport, fish were the very fabric of our lives. Cod, haddock, pollock—these were the heroes of our local lore and economy. We chased, caught, cooked, and dreamed of the bounty of the North Atlantic. Salmon, however, were a distant whisper, fish rarely seen or discussed because, sadly, they had long ceased to be commercially viable in New England.

It wasn't until a few years later, my professional skills honed by culinary school and the intense pressure and precision demanded as a member of the 1992 U.S. Culinary Olympic Team, that I truly encountered salmon in its full glory. A teammate transformed wild king salmon into a gold-medal masterpiece—watching him was a revelation. The texture, the richness, the possibilities: It was unlike any fish I had worked with before. This spark ignited a passion, serendipitously leading me to collaborate with a nascent organization from Europe charged with the promotion of farmed salmon to chefs here in the United States. Suddenly, I was immersed in the world of farmed Atlantic salmon, tasked with demonstrating its quality and versatility nationally. The magnificent fish they sent fueled my curiosity, and trips to the pristine fjords of Norway opened my eyes to the intricacies of aquaculture.

That was over three decades ago. Since then, my fascination has only deepened, evolving into a global pursuit. My work has taken me from the bustling markets of Asia to the rugged coasts of Europe and the complex processing and supply chain for salmon woven across the United States. These past ten years, in particular, have been extraordinary as I've worked in collaboration with some of the leading salmon farmers in Chile, who have treated me like family while sharing access to their farms and technology at a level for which I will always be grateful.

I've spent countless hours developing recipes, researching consumer habits, delving into the science of salmonids (members of the Salmonidae family), and collaborating with experts. It is this cumulative experience—as a chef driven by flavor and technique; an educator committed to clarity and understanding; a competitor who strives for excellence; and a lifelong student of the sea—that I bring to you in this book.

The Complete Guide to Salmon is the culmination of my journey, designed to be the definitive resource for the home cook and novice professional alike. I seek to demystify the world of salmon, starting with its rise to global prominence and the compelling health benefits it offers. Then I delve into the essential "technical stuff": understanding the biology and life cycle, differentiating between the eight common species, and critically examining the distinctions, benefits, and challenges of wild, hatchery wild, and farmed salmon.

Readers will gain the confidence required to navigate the supermarket fish counter, understanding different cuts and how to select the best-quality fish. At the start of each chapter cooking methods are discussed, from achieving the perfect sear or gentle poach to mastery of curing and raw preparations that are safe to eat and delicious.

Aerial image of the Medvejie Salmon Hatchery located at the eastern end of Silver Bay just outside Sitka, Alaska. Medvejie is known for being Alaska's most valuable hatchery chinook contributor.

The recipes in this cookbook span the globe and are informed by my travels and experience, as well as by the assistance and insight shared by the many professional chefs I've worked with in my career.

My goal is not just to provide recipes, but to empower you with knowledge. This book aims to foster a deeper appreciation for salmon—understanding its journey from ocean to plate, recognizing the importance of sustainable practices, and, ultimately, enabling you to unlock the full, delicious promise of salmon in your own kitchen. Whether you're cooking salmon for the first time or seeking to refine your technique, consider this your complete and trusted guide. Now, let's head to the kitchen and dive in.

WHAT IS SALMON?

Salmon is one of the most popular fish consumed in the world. But to define salmon merely as "fish" is to overlook a narrative of ecological wonder, biological distinction, and profound culinary significance. It is an ingredient that bridges wild, untamed ecosystems with the carefully managed environments of modern aquaculture, requiring a nuanced understanding from culinary professionals and home cooks. All salmon belong to the family Salmonidae. They are finfish found in tributaries of the North Atlantic (genus *Salmo*) and Pacific (genus *Oncorhynchus*) Oceans.

Salmon are a marvel of the natural world. Their life cycle is the stuff of legend: Originally hatched in freshwater rivers, often high in mountainous terrain, they migrate downstream to the vastness of the ocean where they spend years foraging and maturing. Then, driven by an immutable instinct, they return, often to the very stream of their birth, battling currents and predators to spawn and complete their cycle. This extraordinary biological journey—the transition between fresh water and salt water and back, the intense physical exertion, and the diverse diet—profoundly impacts these fish. The flesh is typically firm, deeply colored, full of flavor, and infused with healthful omega-3 fatty acids—characteristics that have fueled consumer demand.

However, the global appetite for salmon far exceeds what wild stocks can provide. This reality has propelled the rise and advancement of aquaculture, making farmed salmon a ubiquitous presence in markets worldwide. Predominantly, this involves Atlantic salmon (*Salmo salar*), cultivated in large net pens in coastal waters across regions like Norway, Chile, Scotland, and Canada, although other species, like coho, steelhead, and king, are also farmed. Aquaculture offers consistency in size, year-round availability, and often a more accessible price point. Farmed salmon typically have a higher fat content due to controlled diets and less strenuous lives, resulting in a milder flavor profile and a more tender texture compared to their wild counterparts. The salmon aquaculture industry is continuously striving for improvements in sustainable feed composition, habitat management, fish welfare, and environmental impact mitigation—all crucial considerations for the responsible chef and consumer.

Understanding the differences between wild and farmed salmon is paramount in the kitchen. The question of which is better depends on the eater. Wild and farmed salmon are different, offering unique characteristics that lend themselves to varied culinary applications. The leaner, intensely flavored flesh of a wild sockeye might be best suited to gentle cooking methods like poaching or quick searing to preserve its texture, while richer, fattier farmed Atlantic salmon can beautifully withstand higher heat applications like grilling or roasting, developing a succulent, flaky result. Its milder taste also makes it an excellent canvas for sauces and bolder flavor pairings. Recognizing the source—wild-caught or farm-raised—allows the discerning cook to make informed decisions that highlight and enhance the specific attributes of the salmon at hand.

Ultimately, salmon, in all its forms, remains a culinary cornerstone. Its nutritional profile is exceptional, its versatility across global cuisines is unmatched—from delicate sashimi to robust smoked preparations—and its vibrant color adds undeniable visual appeal. It is an ingredient that carries stories of epic migrations, human ingenuity in aquaculture, ecological balance, and culinary tradition. To truly master salmon is to appreciate this depth, respecting both the wild and the cultivated resource, and applying skill and knowledge to unlock its magnificent deliciousness.

SALMON'S RISE TO PROMINENCE

Salmon's popularity in the United States has surged dramatically in recent years. It currently holds the top spot when it comes to fish species (and second place as the most consumed seafood overall, only surpassed by shrimp). In fact, salmon accounts for approximately 14 percent of all fish consumed in the United States. Though not the highest when it comes to per capita consumption compared to other countries like Japan, the US is the largest overall consumer of salmon in the world. This surge can be attributed to several factors. As information about the nutritional value of salmon and its positive impact on health becomes more widespread, consumers are increasingly incorporating it into their diets. In today's fast-paced world, people are seeking convenient yet healthy meal solutions. Salmon fits the bill perfectly, offering a balance of nutrition and ease of preparation. However, this increasing demand for salmon raises concerns about the future of the market. Experts predict that demand might outpace production growth in the coming years, highlighting the need for sustainable fishing and farming practices to ensure the long-term availability of this valuable resource.

WHY WE EAT SALMON

Today, the drivers of salmon consumption are preference for the taste and texture followed by availability and then the overall health benefits. When it comes to availability, salmon has become the "fourth" protein of grocery retail along with chicken, pork, and beef. It is the primary driver of sales at the fresh seafood counter in your local supermarket. In recent years, research confirming the health benefits associated with consumption of oily fish like salmon has proliferated and caused consumption to spike. Salmon now has a health "halo," making it the healthiest of the other three protein types it competes against—far ahead of beef and pork, in particular.

When people say that salmon is a healthy food, it isn't hyperbole. Strong scientific data supports the claim. So much so that salmon is specifically recognized as a healthy food by our government. The Food and Drug Administration (FDA) determines how and when the term "healthy" can be used as a claim on the labeling of food products to help consumers identify nutritious foods that, when consumed, are consistent with dietary recommendations. The FDA ensures that the labels on food products are truthful and not deceptive.

People ask me what the specific health benefits of salmon consumption are. I'm quick to summarize the cardiovascular, brain, and cognitive benefits, as well as associated anti-inflammatory effects. Few foods are as nutrient-laden.

OPPOSITE: Atlantic salmon smolt at the Salmones Camanchaca hatchery adjacent to the Petrohué River, just east of Puerto Varas in Los Lagos, Chile.

HEALTH BENEFITS OF SALMON CONSUMPTION

Here's a quick list:

OMEGA-3 FATTY ACIDS: These heart-healthy fats are crucial for brain function, reducing inflammation, and lowering the risk of heart disease. Studies have shown that consuming omega-3s can significantly improve heart function and lower blood pressure. Studies also show that the optimal way to consume omega-3s is through consumption of foods like salmon rather than supplements.

Generally speaking, U.S. Department of Agriculture (USDA) data suggests that farmed salmon tends to be higher in overall omega-3 fatty acids than wild salmon. Farmed salmon are fed a controlled diet that is steady in fat content and includes omega-3-rich ingredients like fish oil or fish meal. These boost the overall fat content and assure the final product found in supermarkets is consistent. Wild salmon, on the other hand, forage for their food and consume a range of wild species that differ in fat content. They also face challenging environmental conditions that require greater physical activity and the burning of fat and energy to survive. Wild salmon don't often have the luxury of growing fat. One additional caveat: While farmed salmon often have higher total omega-3s, they also often have higher omega-6 fatty acids, which can be less beneficial for overall health if the omega-3 to omega-6 ratio is too high. Wild salmon typically have a more favorable omega-3 to omega-6 ratio.

HIGH-QUALITY PROTEIN: Salmon is packed with protein, essential for building and repairing tissues, maintaining healthy bones, and preserving muscle mass. A 3-ounce serving provides around 22 grams of protein.

B VITAMINS: Salmon is a rich source of various B vitamins, including B12, niacin, and B6, which are vital for energy production, DNA repair, and brain health. Notably, salmon, especially wild-caught varieties, is one of the few natural food sources of vitamin D, which is crucial for many Americans who may be deficient in this essential vitamin.

VITAMIN D: Depending on the species, a 4-ounce portion of salmon can provide anywhere from one-quarter to three-quarters of the 600 IU recommended daily intake. Vitamin D helps your body absorb calcium, which is essential for building and maintaining strong bones. It also plays a key role in supporting a healthy immune system, helping your body fight off infections and disease.

POTASSIUM: This mineral helps regulate blood pressure and prevents fluid retention. Wild salmon is a particularly good source of potassium, providing 13 percent of the daily value per 3.5-ounce serving.

SELENIUM: This mineral is important for thyroid function, bone health, and protection against certain cancers. A 3.5-ounce serving of salmon provides 75 to 85 percent of the daily value of selenium.

ASTAXANTHIN: This powerful antioxidant contributes to heart, brain, and skin health. It's also what gives salmon its characteristic bright orange color, though some self-proclaimed pundits falsely claim that the astaxanthin added to farmed salmon feed is detrimental (calling it a dye to attract attention and scare people).

SALMON: THE TECHNICAL STUFF

PECTORAL FINS: Create lift and help the fish turn left or right

PELVIC FINS: Help with stability and to slow them down; they can also help the fish move up or down in the water

ANAL FIN: Stabilizes and helps control roll

CAUDAL FIN: The tail fin provides propulsion and speed. In females it is used to dig what is called a "redd," a nest in the gravel of a stream where eggs are laid and incubated. Salmon born in hatcheries often have this fin removed to distinguish them from wild fish when caught.

ADIPOSE FIN: Researchers are unsure of what this fin is used for, but data suggests it acts as a sensor to detect water flow ahead of the caudal fin.

DORSAL FIN: Helps prevent roll and allows quick stops and turns

LATERAL LINE: Composed of cells that detect sound waves and vibrations, pressure, and movement in the water

OPERCULUM: Covers the gill filaments and forces water and oxygen over the gills

EYE: Provides sharp vision under water; each eye can swivel independently of each other

NOSTRILS: Provide a deep sense of smell and help salmon navigate back to streams where they were born to spawn

MOUTH: Helps take in food and forces water over gills to supply oxygen

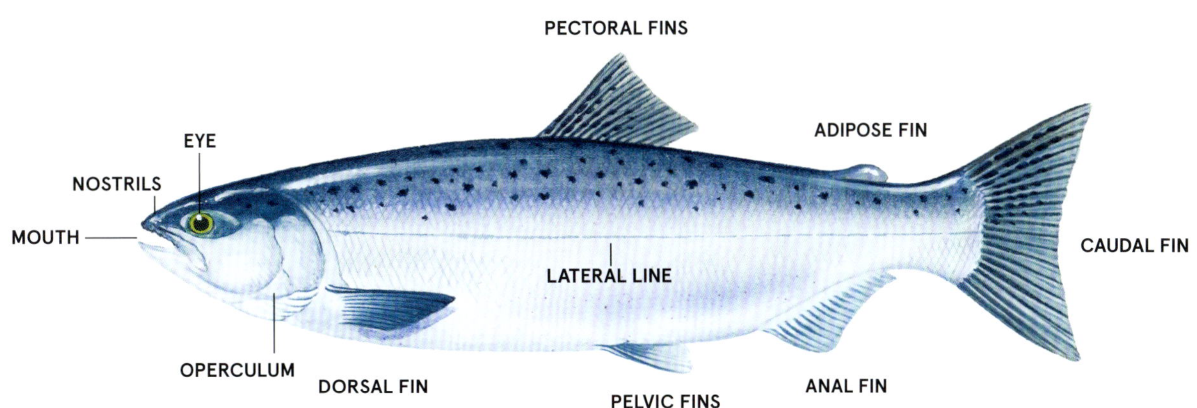

ABOUT THE PARTS WE EAT

Salmon have two major muscle groups: epaxial and hypaxial. The **epaxial muscle** (what chefs call the loin) runs along the upper or top half, or dorsal side, of the fish from head to tail. **Hypaxial muscles** (what chefs call the belly) are located along the ventral or bottom half of the fish from just behind the gill, flowing around the abdominal cavity to the tail. These muscle groups are the ones used to create swimming motion. The clusters on one side of the fish contract while the opposite side relaxes, allowing the fish to undulate from side to side while motoring through the water.

A BIT OF SALMON SCIENCE

From a technical perspective, salmon is a generic name for three genera of fish that are native to tributaries of the North Atlantic (genus *Salmo*) the North Pacific (genus *Oncorhynchus*), or are circumpolar in habitat, including both the Atlantic and Pacific (genus *Salvelinus*). The Pacific salmon species, king (Chinook), sockeye (red), coho (silver), pink (humpback), and chum (keta) salmon, along with rainbow (steelhead) trout, are the most sold of genus *Oncorhynchus*. Atlantic salmon are the most sold North Atlantic species of the genus *Salmo*. The third species is arctic char, which falls under the genus *Salvelinus*. All are of the family Salmonidae, and all are euryhaline, meaning they can survive and thrive in a wide range of salinities, including both freshwater and saltwater environments.

EIGHT COMMON SALMON SPECIES

To keep things simple, the summary below starts with wild salmon, while including hatchery salmon where appropriate, then follows with a summary of farmed salmon. Wild and hatchery salmon are seasonal, from roughly April to early October each year, though frozen products are available year-round. The primary wild or hatchery species sold in the US are from the Pacific and include king, sockeye, coho, pink, and chum.

1. KING SALMON/CHINOOK (*ONCORHYNCHUS TSHAWYTSCHA*):

Mostly wild. Fresh harvest season is year-round, though the peak for fresh is May through July. The average size is 36 inches. Identifying features: Black mouth and gum line, dark spots on back and tail. Performance: The high oil content in these fish make them harder to overcook.

This species is rich in omega-3 fatty acids, large in size, and often the most expensive fresh salmon sold at your local retailer. Though other species of wild salmon are best when cooked to a lower temperature, king salmon can withstand a higher temperature doneness of 124 to 126°F due to size and fat content. In the wild, this salmon has a range from the Central Coast of California all the way north to the coast of mid-Alaska and east to Asia. Most of the king salmon sold in the US is wild, though there are companies successfully farming king salmon in the Southern Hemisphere.

VARIETIES OF KING SALMON:

IVORY KING SALMON: Ivory kings have a recessive gene that prevents them from converting astaxanthin, the compound that gives salmon its bright orange color. Pigment fails to deposit in their flesh; the result is an ivory-white color.

MARBLE KING SALMON: Marble kings also have a recessive gene that prevents them from converting astaxanthin, but the recessive gene is less pronounced, resulting in a partial ability to convert color. Thus, the flesh is marbled with both ivory and orange coloration.

2. SOCKEYE/RED OR BLUEBACK (*ONCORHYNCHUS NERKA*)

Mostly wild. Fresh harvest season is May through September. The average size is 24 inches. Identifying features: Large, bright, gold-colored eyes, bluish coloring on the top of back, no spots on back, fine speckling on the back, thin tail stock, no dark trim around fins or tail. Performance: The high oil content in these fish make them harder to overcook, but they aren't as high in fat as king, so be careful.

Sockeye is also a delicious wild salmon option. Flesh color is a deep ruby red due to the higher percentage of crustaceans and plankton these fish consume. Due to their lower fat content, sockeye are more sensitive to overcooking and tend to have a stronger flavor. Sockeye sources like the Columbia River in Washington and the Copper River in Alaska are highly prized, and the fish are branded by location, resulting in higher prices and demand, particularly among chefs. Cook to 122°F in most cases.

3. COHO/SILVER (*ONCORHYNCHUS KISUTCH*)

Wild, hatchery, farmed. Fresh harvest season is end of July to mid-December. The average size is 24 to 36 inches. Identifying features: White gums, dark spots on back, spots on upper tail only, large scales. Performance: The medium oil content in these fish makes them slightly harder to cook, so be careful not to overcook.

Coho hatch in fresh water and stay for two years before transitioning to the ocean, where they live for two years and then return back to fresh water to spawn. The flesh color is a moderate orange. The species is lighter in color, lower in fat content, and smaller in size, though they can grow as large as 36 inches. The flavor is mild, and this fish is often more affordable when sold fresh at the grocery store. Like sockeye, this species is better when cooked to 122°F if wild, due to its low fat content; 124°F if farmed.

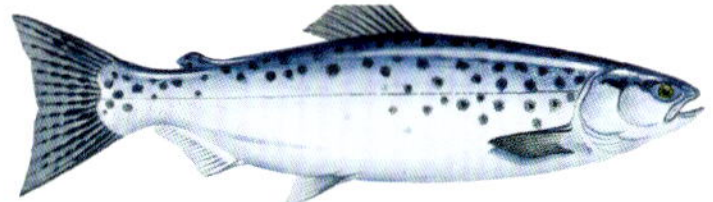

4. PINK/HUMPBACK (*ONCORHYNCHUS GORBUSCHA*):

Wild and hatchery. Fresh harvest season is June through early September. The average size is 20 to 25 inches. Identifying features: White mouth with black gum line, small teeth, small loosely set scales, large black spots on back, large oval spots on tail. Performance: The lower oil content in these fish causes them to cook and dry out faster. The finished product is lean and delicate with a mild flake and flavor. Cook carefully to preserve quality.

Most of the pink salmon consumed start the first years of their lives in a farm. The fish are small, often between 2 and 6 pounds. In addition to fresh and frozen products, this fish is often canned or packed in aseptic pouches for retail sale. This species is better when cooked to 122°F.

PERIODIC TABLE OF SALMON

Salmon	Omega-3 Levels*	Season Fresh	Price	Flavor, Texture, Flake
Atlantic *Salmo salar* (Fresh, Frozen, Farmed)	♥♥♥♥♥	FARMED YEAR-ROUND	$$	Buttery Rich Flavor, Firm and Fatty, Medium-Large Flake
King/Chinook *Oncorhynchus tshawytscha* (Fresh, Frozen, Wild, Farmed)	♥♥♥♥♥	LIMITED YEAR-ROUND, PEAK MAY–JULY	$$$$$	Rich Flavor, Moderately Firm Texture, Large Flake
Arctic Char *Salvelinus alpinus* (Fresh, Frozen, Farmed)	♥♥½	FARMED YEAR-ROUND	$$$	Mild Flavor, Medium Texture, Small Flake
Coho/Silver *Oncorhynchus kisutch* (Fresh, Frozen, Wild, Farmed)	♥♥½	JULY–DECEMBER	$$	Mild Flavor, Firm and Fatty, Medium Flake
Sockeye/Red or Blueback *Oncorhynchus nerka* (Fresh, Frozen, Canned, Wild)	♥♥½	MAY–SEPTEMBER	$$$	Rich Flavor, Firm Texture, Medium-Large Flake
Steelhead/Rainbow Trout *Oncorhynchus mykiss* (Fresh, Frozen, Wild, Farmed)	♥♥½	FARMED YEAR-ROUND	$$	Mild Flavor, Medium Texture, Small Flake
Chum/Keta *Oncorhynchus keta* (Fresh, Frozen, Wild)	♥½	JUNE–MID-OCTOBER	$$	Mild Flavor, Firm Texture, Medium Flake
Pink/Humpback *Oncorhynchus gorbuscha* (Fresh, Frozen, Canned, Wild)	♥½	JUNE–SEPTEMBER	$	Mild Flavor, Soft Texture, Small Flake

Fresh · Frozen · Canned · W Wild · F Farmed

OMEGA-3 LEVELS GUIDE*

♥	400–800 mg
♥♥	801–1200 mg
♥♥♥	1201–1600 mg
♥♥♥♥	1601–2000 mg
♥♥♥♥♥	> 2001 mg

PRICING GUIDE

$	$5–8/lb
$$	$9–12/lb
$$$	$13–16/lb
$$$$	$17–20/lb
$$$$$	> $21/lb

* The omega-3 information provided is based on the following: National Institutes of Health-Office of Dietary Supplements, Omega-3 Fatty Acids: Fact Sheet for Health Professionals, December 12, 2020; Penny M. Kris-Etherton, William S. Harris, and Lawrence J. Appel, "Fish Consumption, Fish Oil, Omega-3 Fatty Acids, and Cardiovascular Disease." *Circulation*, no. 106 (Philadelphia: Lippincott Williams & Wilkins for the American Heart Association, November 19, 2002).

5. CHUM/KETA (*ONCORHYNCHUS KETA*):

Wild and hatchery. Fresh harvest season is end of June to mid-October. The average size is 24 to 28 inches. Identifying features: White mouth and gum line, no spots on back or tail, fine speckling on the back, dark trim on fins and tail. Performance: The low oil content in these fish makes them harder to cook, so be very careful not to overcook.

This is the least prized of the five main species of salmon produced in the wild. Gutted fish are typically between 7 to 9 pounds and shaped like footballs. Fillets are light pink in color and very mild in flavor. When sold fresh, this is usually the cheapest species at the grocery store. In the kitchen, chum is best when cooked to 122°F. At lower doneness they retain a succulent texture and better flavor.

6. STEELHEAD/RAINBOW TROUT (*ONCORHYNCHUS MYKISS*):

Mostly farmed. Available fresh year-round. The average size is 24 to 28 inches. Identifying features: Small black spots on back, sides, and tail, bluish-gray back, and bright silvery sides. Performance: The high oil content in these fish makes them easier to cook and very similar to farmed Atlantic and coho salmon.

This mostly farmed species is growing in popularity. These fish are small at 2 to 3 pounds, firm in texture while mild in flavor, and low in omega-3 fatty acids. The color can range from pink to bright orange. Most of the steelhead sold in the US are farmed both domestically and abroad (primarily Chile). Wild steelheads are available on a limited, highly seasonal basis in the Pacific Northwest. Cook to 124°F for best results.

7. ATLANTIC (*SALMO SALAR*):

Mostly farmed. Available fresh year-round. As noted earlier, Atlantic salmon is the largest and fastest-growing type of salmon sold in the US. The main reason this species has such large market share is the history of *Salmo salar* husbandry, which dates to the mid-nineteenth century. Atlantic salmon are dark (blue-green) along the top of their back and have shiny silver sides. Their spots are black and tend to be X- or Y-shaped, mainly above the lateral half of their body including along the top of the head to the gill plate. Their caudal (tail) fin is usually slightly forked or indented. Atlantic salmon is the largest and fastest-growing type of salmon sold in the US. The main reason farmed Atlantic salmon has thrived in Norway, Scotland, the Faroe Islands, Iceland, Canada, and Chile. Farmed Atlantic salmon is available fresh and frozen year-round. Fillets are mild in flavor, consistent in size and color, and have the highest levels of omega-3 fatty acids of all salmon. Cook to 124°F for best results.

8. ARCTIC CHAR (*SALVELINUS ALPINUS*):

Mostly farmed. Available year-round. Identifying features: Round, red, pink, or yellow spots on sides, tail slightly forked; eight to twelve anal fin rays; no dark-green wavy marks on back or dorsal fin. Farmed Arctic Char sold in the US, primarily from Canada and Iceland, offers a delicate, mild flavor, often described as a cross between salmon and trout, with a rich, flaky, pink-orange flesh. Cook to 124°F for best results.

THREE TYPES OF SALMON: WILD, HATCHERY WILD & FARMED

Most salmon-loving consumers believe there are just two types: farmed and wild. In fact, there are three origins of salmon sold in the US: wild salmon, hatchery wild salmon, and farmed salmon. Wild salmon exists purely in the wild, as nature intended, without any human intervention or support. These fish come almost exclusively from the Pacific Ocean and include multiple species like king, sockeye, coho, pink, and chum.

Hatchery wild salmon are fish that begin their lives in hatcheries using eggs and milts harvested from returning wild salmon. They grow to smolt while reared in captivity before being released into the wild. Once released, these fish grow to maturity in the northern Pacific Ocean before returning to where they were released. Hundreds of millions of fish are released from hatcheries in Alaska, Russia, and Japan to enhance wild populations. Though most folks in the US are aware of wild and farmed, few consumers are aware of the broad category of hatchery wild fish sold. Wild fish that are partially reared in captivity are never labeled as such in the US—they are sold as identical to their truly wild cousins. Consumers who claim to only consume wild salmon often consume fish that are, in fact, partially farmed.

The third and most common type of salmon sold in the US is farmed; these fish start and end their life cycles in captivity. A vast majority is Atlantic salmon farmed in Chile, Norway, Canada, Scotland, the Faroe Islands, and Iceland.

WILD SALMON

It's four a.m. in Seattle at the end of June, and I'm up early with my son headed north to Edmonds to meet a charter boat captain for a daylong adventure in pursuit of king salmon on Puget Sound. We plan to set out from the marina and then motor due west with our trolls out to Appletree Cove. From there, we will head southeast to just off of Richmond Park Beach and then back to Edmonds. It's early in the season yet, but the weather is good, and the fishing reports indicate that a fair number of local king salmon are being caught that comply with catch regulations. These fish are known as "black mouth" salmon—immature hatchery fish native to the Sound that haven't departed for the open ocean or matured enough to spawn. We aren't 15 minutes out of Edmonds in a light chop, with the sun poking over the horizon, when I hear a click on the reel to my right. Then another click. My heart starts to race—we're on. The wild salmon fun begins.

Wild salmon are found in lakes, rivers, streams, and the ocean throughout the temperate regions of the Northern Hemisphere, including North America, Europe, and Asia. However, all things aren't equal from one ocean to another. The northern Pacific Ocean still maintains robust populations of wild salmon, but the North Atlantic does not. Wild Atlantic salmon populations have been depleted from decades of overfishing. Remaining wild stocks are highly regulated from the coast of Norway to Iceland, Canada, and the northeast coast of the US. In most places it is illegal to commercially fish for wild Atlantic salmon. The northern Pacific Ocean is a different story—wild stocks remain commercially viable. Commercial wild salmon fisheries are active from the northern part of the Sea of Japan (East Sea) to the Sea of Okhotsk, along the east coast of Russia, north to the ice-cold Bering Sea, farther east to the Gulf of Alaska, and south along the Pacific Coast to Monterey Bay, California.

Russia remains a powerhouse source for wild salmon and accounts for approximately half of the global harvest. The US is second with approximately one-third of the harvest. Japan and Canada round out the top four. In the US, the

Wild salmon on display at the Pike Place Market in Seattle, Washington.

salmon harvest is measured in two ways: by total fish caught and by market value.

Since salmon are temperature-sensitive, wild salmon were never able to migrate far enough south to populate the Southern Hemisphere due to thermal barriers and changing ocean conditions. However, "wild" salmon are now found in the Southern Hemisphere. King salmon were introduced to rivers in New Zealand in the early nineteenth century and salmonids were introduced in the Patagonia region of South America in the early twentieth century for recreational fishing purposes. In both instances, these non-native species were released into local rivers and streams with the intention of establishing populations that could support recreational fishing and tourism. Later, in the 1970s, king salmon (Chinook) eggs and alevins from Washington State were released into rivers in the Patagonia region of Chile for the same purpose. Recent genetic studies of king salmon around the Petrohué River basin in Chile show that these fish established and are still present. Though introduced in prior decades, these fish are now considered wild.

Whether truly wild or previously stocked and now considered wild, most of these fish are anadromous, spending parts of their lives in both fresh and salt water. Their early lives are spent in fresh water, then they migrate to the ocean until maturity and return to fresh water (rivers and streams) late in life to spawn. The Southern Hemisphere fish are mostly caught for recreational purposes. Northern Hemisphere fish in the Pacific Ocean are just the opposite—they are subject to heavy commercial fishing.

Human intervention only occurs toward the end of the maturation process. Wild salmon are caught as their natural life cycles in the wild come to an end. Commercial fishers use various harvest techniques, including gillnets, purse seines, trawling, and longlines using hooks and bait or lures. The catch method depends on the individual species and habitat.

King salmon fishing in a light chop on Puget Sound off Edmonds, Washington.

GILLNET FISHING: A gillnet is a curtain-type net designed to entangle targeted fish species by their gills. It floats in the water column and generally avoids direct contact with the seabed, reducing potential bycatch of nontargeted species.

PURSE SEINE FISHING: Uses a long, vertical net, often referred to as a "curtain," to encircle schools of salmon. Once a school is surrounded, a line threaded through the bottom of the net is drawn tight, much like the drawstring of a purse. This action closes the bottom of the net, trapping the fish inside.

LONGLINE FISHING: Involves deploying a main fishing line, often miles long, that trails behind a boat. Shorter lines, called snoods, are attached at intervals along the main line, each fitted with a baited hook. This method targets salmon swimming at specific depths. To minimize potential bycatch, fishers often use specific gear modifications, fishing practices, and deterrents.

HATCHERY WILD SALMON

Tucked away in Issaquah, Washington, is a fantastic salmon hatchery and visitors center, owned and operated by the Washington State Department of Fish & Wildlife (WDFW). The Issaquah Salmon Hatchery was constructed in 1936 as part of the federal Works Progress Administration program and has operated ever since. It is the most-visited hatchery in the state, set below verdant rolling hills and small mountains lush with Douglas fir and western hemlock. The day I visit, the facility isn't running at full capacity, though there are coho salmon in the raceways on the southwest corner of the property.

There are more than one hundred hatcheries in Washington State, run by the state government, the federal government, or Indigenous tribes. Without them, the wild salmon populations would be in deep trouble: Hatcheries are critical to the long-term viability of salmon in the region.

A salmon hatchery is a facility where salmon are raised in a controlled setting from egg to smolt and then released into the wild or, in the case of farmed salmon, a controlled grow-out facility or cage until harvest. These facilities operate as both a marine laboratory and a farm, where fish roe (eggs) and milt (sperm) are gathered from select fish, then mixed and fertilized in a lab-like setting. Once fertilized, the embryos are placed in incubators until they hatch, and the hatchlings are cared for through all stages of development until ready for release or grow-out.

The very first hatchery was established in Maine in 1871 to improve wild Atlantic salmon runs in New England. Just twenty years later, in 1891, the first commercial salmon hatchery in Alaska was launched to enhance sockeye salmon populations. Hatcheries have been in use ever since.

Like most methods of captive breeding, hatchery-reared salmon are released into the wild once they complete their freshwater juvenile life stage. Juvenile fish in hatcheries are reared in a stable, man-made environment with abundant food and no predators.

The Alaska hatchery plan in use today was designed to enhance overall fisheries, increase the quantity of wild salmon, and reduce pressure on wild stocks. It began in 1971, after a historically low salmon harvest one year earlier in 1970. From the beginning, the plan intended to supplement natural production, not replace or displace it. By most measures, the plan has been a success. Alaska commercial salmon harvests have improved since the plan was implemented.

Today, thirty hatcheries operate in Alaska; twenty-six are operated by private nonprofit organizations. Alaska's Department of Fish and Game considers both naturally propagating and hatchery salmon to be wild.

HATCHERY AND WILD SALMON INTERACTION

Researchers have been tracking the impact of hatchery salmon on wild populations for decades. Since the start of hatchery expansion in the late 1970s, concerns over the impact that hatchery fish have on wild populations and ecosystems have persisted. Though there is no question there is an impact, the extent of the impact remains a pertinent question. Persistent efforts are made to keep hatchery fish from negatively impacting wild populations.

When hatchery fish are released into the wild, they generally have reduced reproductive success and decreased survival rates compared to their wild counterparts, due to the way they were raised prior to release. Wild (non-hatchery) salmon undergo natural selection, where weaker individuals are less likely to survive and reproduce. This same selective pressure is largely absent when salmon are raised in a hatchery. If hatchery-reared individuals interbreed with wild individuals there is potential for weaker genetic sets to be propagated. Researchers have found that large releases of hatchery salmonids are likely to trigger adverse impact on comingling populations of wild salmonids. These impacts include reduced survival, growth, reproductive success, and body size.

The Puelo River valley in northern Patagonia is a place rich with Pacific salmon introduced from North America in the 1920s.

SEPARATING HATCHERY FISH FROM WILD

Over the years biologists have figured out creative ways to mark hatchery salmon so they can be tracked and counted. Hatcheries are able to mark the fish they raise using otolith marking or wire tags that are coded. Between these two methods, the accuracy of estimating harvest is fairly precise.

FARMED SALMON

I am out the door at five a.m., this time to meet our helicopter pilot Jaime at Aeródromo El Mirador in Puerto Varas, Chile. Jaime is a salty septuagenarian with decades of experience in fixed and rotary-wing aircraft. He flies a stout and super-reliable Eurocopter AS350 with five seats and a strong payload. Today we are headed out to survey a number of Patagonian salmon-farming sites and the surrounding countryside. First, we will fly northeast to the edge of Mount Osorno—an active volcano—and then farther east to Lake Todos los Santos (All Saints) before pitching south to estuary Reloncavi to do an aerial audit of the salmon-farming sites tucked close to the shore. This northern part of Chile is stunning. So beautifully green and lush with one major exception: There's nothing here. There are only 1.2 million people living in the three southernmost states in Chile (Los Lagos, Aysén, Magallanes) that span one thousand miles from my location in Puerto Varas to the southern town of Punta Arenas, located along the ice-cold and crystal-clear Strait of Magellan near the very tip of South America. Most of these people (well over nine hundred thousand) live in Los Lagos, leaving the two southern states free of people, development, and pollution. I've never seen such pristine wilderness in my life. Jaime will be showing us places that can't be accessed via any other mode of transport than a helicopter. The motor roars, blades start to spin, and we're off, zooming over the cool Patagonia morning air as the sun rises.

I'll admit right up front that I am a big fan of farmed salmon. This doesn't mean that salmon farming is without periodic issues or concerns. But the industry as a whole plays a hugely important role in our food system and, more important, a vital role in the local economies where these facilities operate. My first foray into the industry was more than thirty years ago in Norway. In recent years, I have visited the Patagonia region of Chile multiple times, getting intimate access to all parts of the farming process. The advanced technology in use and the deep community commitment of these farmers is clear.

The farming of fish is an ancient practice that, according to evidence, appears to date back more than eight thousand years to Ancient China. Recently, an international team of researchers analyzed fish bones excavated from the Early Neolithic Jiahu site in Henan Province. Henan is often recognized as the place where Chinese civilization began. Evidence suggests many ancient forms of food production occurred in the region, including the cultivation of common carp (*Cyprinus carpio*). These early forms of fish farming, or what is now called aquaculture, occurred inland and were of the freshwater type.

The US National Oceanographic and Atmospheric Administration defines aquaculture as the breeding, rearing, and harvesting of fish, shellfish, algae, and other organisms in all types of water environments. Aquaculture appears to have started as a freshwater process that eventually expanded to include marine cultivation in salt water.

Early evidence of saltwater aquaculture can be found about 2,500 years ago in Ancient Rome. The Romans farmed oysters and fish in Mediterranean lagoons following techniques that remained largely unchanged until the twentieth century. Mussel farming was developed in the thirteenth century and continues to this day. Carp cultivation expanded in Europe during the Renaissance, particularly in Eastern Europe, using many of the same systems that first propagated in Jiahu several thousand years earlier. Records indicated that Holy Roman Emperor Charles IV of Bohemia ordered the construction of fish ponds at multiple sites back in the fourteenth century.

MODERN SALMON FARMING

Our current form of domesticated salmon originated in Norway in the 1950s. Researchers attribute the start of modern salmon farming to the Vik brothers, who in 1959 launched floating wooden cages that yielded forty mature salmon after a three-year cycle. Up to this point, governments and communities had invested in salmon husbandry to help populate rivers and streams to strengthen recovery of salmon populations—a process that continues in the Pacific Northwest and Alaska. Once it became possible to raise salmon to maturity in captivity, it was only natural for people to consider cultivating salmon for sale. With growth in Norway came the need for oversight by government authorities. The Norwegians formalized regulation in the Aquaculture Act of 1981, which promulgated policies driven by local ownership of small-scale, widely dispersed producers. Regulators considered salmon cultivation a complementary way of generating income for coastal communities. In 1985, the act was updated to remove the local ownership clause but otherwise maintained limits to growth. Though the intent of Norwegian regulation was admirable, the unintended consequence was entrepreneurial interest in pursuit of industrial-scale salmon cultivation outside of Norway. Thus, the industry began its global expansion, in part as a by-product of Norwegian regulation. In the mid-1980s, Scotland, Chile, and Canada were seeded with Norwegian technology and investment in pursuit of the industrial growth that Norway was unwilling to support.

In the late 1980s, the growth of salmon cultivation further accelerated because of advances in feed production, brood stock through selective breeding, equipment and facilities, and fish welfare through creation of vaccines to combat a growing number of illnesses. Global production of salmon then grew too fast, resulting in supply exceeding demand and claims of unfair trade practices on the part of Norway. By February 1990, the US Department of Commerce received a petition from the Coalition for Fair Atlantic Salmon Trade, composed of US producers of Atlantic salmon. The petition eventually resulted in a 2.45-percent tariff on imported Norwegian salmon commencing at the end of June that summer. The industry was in turmoil, and this resulted in a rapid shift in Norwegian regulation and removal of restrictions and barriers to growth. The growth and concentration of ownership seen today was seeded during the economic downcycle and reduced regulation in the early 1990s.

Unlike terrestrial farming, salmon aquaculture is inherently mobile. This includes mobility of brood stock, equipment technology, expertise, capital investment, feed, and vaccines. Though the process of cultivating salmon is easily exported, local communities have tremendous sway on how farming practices evolve once they have started.

Advances in salmon farming have resulted in one of the most efficient feed ratios of all protein categories. For every 1.3 pounds of feed Atlantic salmon consume, they typically yield 1 pound of flesh for a feed ratio of 1.3:1.

The use of pharmacological treatments during cultivation is a concern. Saltwater net pens also cause buildup of refuse on the ocean bottom (below the pens), which requires careful management and fallow periods to allow the natural environment to cleanse itself. But due to rapid increases in global production, farmed Atlantic salmon is generally more affordable than wild or hatchery fish. In nearly all cases, the benefits far outweigh the costs.

Over the past twenty years, farmed salmon has become one of the most popular fish species in the world—and the most popular in the US. However, few people have a sound understanding of how salmon is farmed.

Salmon farmers employ advanced technology and innovation, deep experience, scientific

A saltwater salmon farm located close to shore in Panitao, in Chilean Patagonia, south of Puerto Montt in Los Lagos, Chile.

principles, and public-private partnerships to deliver fresh, healthy, and responsibly raised salmon. The industry is guided by a shared understanding that responsible practices are vital to environmental and organizational health, and industry success. Member organizations strive to meet national and international quality, food safety, environmental, and occupational health and safety standards. The industry is committed to continuous improvement today and in the future.

There are multiple reasons to support farmed salmon. The four reasons here are a start:

1. Farmed salmon is a healthy source of protein. Nearly a decade ago, USDA researchers showed that eating even 4 ounces of farmed Atlantic salmon twice a week raises omega-3s to levels associated with reduced heart disease risk. USDA Dietary Guidelines for Americans recommend seafood consumption at least twice a week.

2. Salmon farming allows for food production in the ocean, which is underutilized. Researchers report that the sea provides only 17 percent of the current production of edible protein. There is an opportunity for salmon farming to help fill the protein gap expected as populations rise and pressure on land sources increases due to climate change—all while reducing pressure on wild seafood.

3. Compared to other proteins like beef, farmed salmon has a low environmental impact and, according to researchers, one of the lowest greenhouse gas profiles of all animal protein sources, offering an eco-friendly alternative.

4. Salmon farming requires far less fresh water. As concerns over water quality and supply grow, it is important to invest in protein sources that have a lower impact on freshwater sources. Salmon is one of these proteins.

THE FARMED SALMON LIFE CYCLE

Farmed salmon, whether Pacific or Atlantic, go through six stages before arriving on the tables of consumers. These stages are highly evolved and include advances in science and technology that have optimized the process.

1. FRESH WATER

MONTH 1: Spawning, fertilization, and incubation: Salmon eggs (ova) are collected from female fish, fertilized, and incubated in fresh water until they hatch.

MONTHS 2 TO 3: Alevins are hatchlings that live off their egg sack in fresh water while they grow.

MONTHS 4 TO 6: Fry are small fish (1 to 2 inches) that are transferred to larger freshwater tanks and feed on their own.

MONTHS 7 TO 9: Parr are larger freshwater fish that rapidly grow and shift in color to silver.

2. BRACKISH WATER

MONTHS 10 TO 12: Smolt are fish that are starting to look like salmon. They shift to dark silver with a spotted black top and undergo smoltification. Smoltification refers to the fish's transition from fresh to salt water. These fish grow to 200 to 300 grams (7 to 10 ounces) before moving to the next stage.

3. SALT WATER: MATURATION AT SEA

MONTHS 13 TO 28: At this stage, smolt are placed in net pens in the ocean and steadily grow as they mature to sizes ranging from 7 to 12 pounds, on average. This process can take from 12 to 28 months.

4. HARVEST

Once harvest weight is achieved, usually 9 to 12 pounds, the salmon are mechanically removed from ocean net pens and transferred to processing facilities.

5. PROCESSING

Processing facilities are meticulously designed to assure optimal quality and efficiency. Facilities are highly automated and efficiently designed to assure safe, humane, and sanitary operation.

Most facilities are certified by the third-party Best Aquaculture Practices and/or Aquaculture Stewardship Council.

6. FINISHED PRODUCT TO END USER

Salmon companies use state-of-the-art packaging, advanced logistics, and a secure cold chain to deliver products to distributors, grocer retailers, and food service in fresh, frozen, bulk, and value-added form.

FROM HARVEST TO GROCERY STORE

The journey of a salmon fillet from a whole fish to your grocery store involves several highly choreographed steps starting with harvest.

1. HARVEST

The harvest method for salmon depends on the species. Once caught, the fish are hauled aboard boats for transport to a processing facility.

Farmed salmon are harvested when they reach market weight. Since most salmon are grown to harvest weight in offshore ocean pens, harvest begins by transferring the fish from the net pen to the well boat. A well boat is a vessel with large onboard tanks designed to transport live salmon to onshore processing facilities. Salmon are moved from the net pen to the well-boat tank and then transported live to a processing facility.

SALMON GROWTH AND HARVEST CYCLE

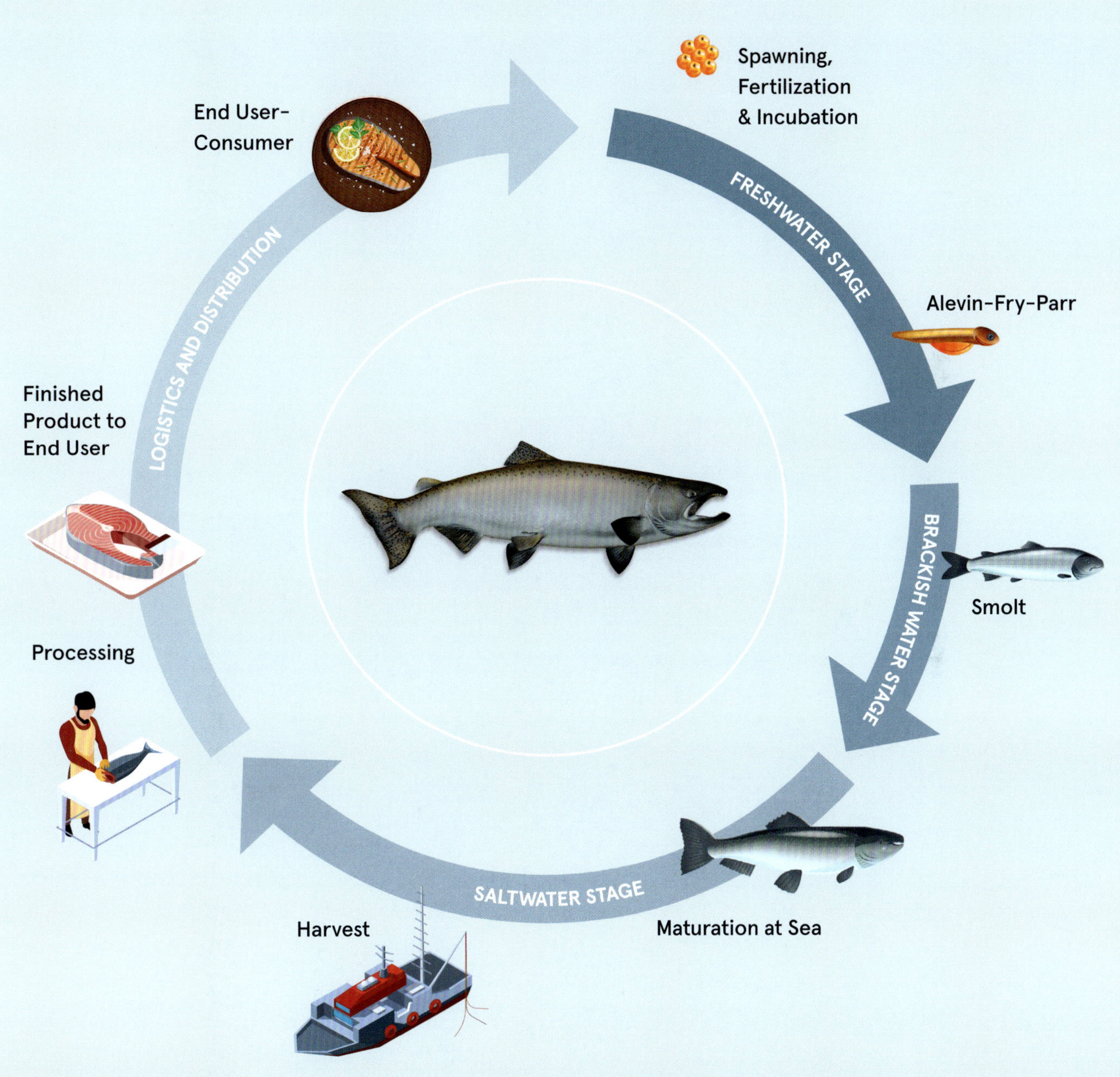

COLLAR
LOIN
BELLY
TAIL

2. PROCESSING

FOR WILD SALMON: Processing begins when the fish are landed on the boat. The fish are gutted and bled immediately. This is crucial for maintaining the quality and freshness of the fish.

FOR FARMED: The fish are conveyed into the facility and processing begins. The first step is to humanely stun the fish rendering it unconscious. This is usually done with a specially designed pneumatic device. Next, the fish are bled and gutted. Then they are rinsed and sanitized and head either to chilling (for whole fish) or to further processing into fillets or portions prior to packaging and chilling or freezing.

3. FILLETING

For this step, both farmed and wild fish travel the same path. Fillets are manually or mechanically removed from the fish. Depending on the specification, the fish will undergo further processing including pinbone removal, skin removal, and additional trimming.

4. PORTIONING

This step involves manual cutting or the use of machines that scan and automatically cut fillets into preprogrammed portion sizes.

5. PACKAGING

As the portions travel down a conveyor, they are sorted and prepped for final packaging.

VACUUM PACKAGING: This involves placing the salmon in a special plastic bag and then using a vacuum sealer to remove all the air before sealing it tightly. Vacuum packaging extends shelf life and minimizes freezer burn. By removing oxygen, it prevents the fish from drying out and developing off-flavors.

INDIVIDUALLY QUICK FROZEN (IQF): Salmon fillets or portions are individually frozen on trays or conveyor belts, ensuring they freeze quickly and don't stick together. They are often glazed with a thin layer of ice for added protection. IQF helps maintain the fish's delicate texture. The frozen salmon is usually packed in plastic bags and stored frozen until transport.

BLOCK FROZEN: Salmon fillets are layered in a container or mold, and then frozen solid into a large block. This maximizes space in commercial freezers. Block freezing is not a common approach for fillets or portions sold at retail. However, this bulk-processing method is not uncommon for smoking, canning, or other value-added products.

Most of the fish you buy is vacuum packaged and shipped fresh or frozen or IQF.

6. SHIPPING

Once the fish is caught, processed, and packaged, it goes into inventory and proceeds through distribution via frozen containers or fresh air freight. Whether fresh or frozen, the fish ends up at grocery retail distribution centers that stage the product for final shipping to your local grocery store. Since fresh salmon is highly perishable, the logistics process has to move quickly and consistently. Any delay can have a major impact on product shelf life and quality.

7. RETAIL MERCHANDISING

Retailers are highly advanced when it comes to the seafood products they sell and the format in which they are sold. Since spoilage is a major cost for the grocery industry, salmon is purchased and merchandised to optimize sales volume and inventory turnover. In other words, your grocery store purchases and displays just the right number of fish to sell quickly during a given week of the year.

PURCHASING SALMON

Shopping for salmon can be confusing. Add in the misinformation traversing social media, and the constant opinions shared by influencers, pundits, and NGOs, and confusion can arise. Regardless of opinions, salmon is a juggernaut, and consumers need guidelines and reassurance at the seafood counter of their local store.

Fillets and, to a lesser extent, steaks are the most common forms of salmon purchased at retail in the US. Thus, finding and buying high-quality salmon is not difficult but does require some thought. Purchasing whole fish is a bit more complicated but far less frequent unless in commercial food service.

FRESH SALMON

When purchasing fresh salmon, take a close look at the fillet itself: It should be vibrant, moist, and firm, never dull, dry, or flaking apart. Next, the smell is crucial; a truly fresh fillet has a clean, subtle scent of the ocean, not an overpowering or ammoniated "fishy" smell. The skin should be bright and scales intact, if present.

The most important considerations when buying fresh salmon:

VIBRANT APPEARANCE AND MOISTURE: Seek bright, consistent color and visibly moist, firm flesh without any browning, gaping, or other signs of dehydration.

CLEAN AROMA: A subtle, fresh, oceanic scent is paramount; the absence of any strong, unpleasant odors is always your best guarantee of freshness.

FROZEN SALMON

When shopping for salmon in the freezer case, packaging is your first clue to quality: It must be tightly vacuum-sealed with no tears or signs of freezer burn (excessive ice inside, white patches on the fish). Look for terms like "IQF" (Individually Quick Frozen), which indicates rapid freezing at peak freshness.

The most important considerations when buying frozen salmon:

PACKAGING INTEGRITY AND FREEZING METHOD: Look for perfectly vacuum-sealed packages with minimal or no ice crystals inside. Seek out "IQF" (Individually Quick Frozen) on the label; this process is is key to preserving texture and flavor during freezing.

ABSENCE OF FREEZER BURN: Visually inspect the fish through the packaging for a vibrant color without white spots, discoloration, or a dried-out appearance, all tell-tale signs of freezer burn that compromises quality.

WHOLE FRESH SALMON

When purchasing whole fresh salmon, examine the fish for clear eyes, bright red gills, shiny skin, firm flesh, and a clean, subtle ocean smell—signs of peak freshness.

The most important considerations when buying fresh whole salmon:

EYES: Bulging, shiny, bright, and clear (not cloudy)

GILLS: Bright red, firm, not slimy or broken

SHINY SKIN: Bright and clear with no fading or dry spots

FIRM FLESH: Skin and flesh firm to the touch

SMELL: Fresh, mild, slight scent of ocean (not fishy), free of ammonia

COMMON RETAIL CUTS OF SALMON

WHOLE FILLET OR SIDE: Refers to an entire half of a salmon with the head, tail, and spine removed. A side of salmon usually includes the skin and may have pinbones toward the thicker (head end) of the fillet. The size of a side of salmon depends on the species: king and Atlantic salmon can range from 2 to 4 pounds per side. Coho and rainbow trout are between 1½ to 3 pounds, and sockeye salmon can be even smaller, averaging 1 to 2 pounds per side. I like purchasing a frozen, vacuum-packaged side of salmon for value.

FILLET PORTIONS: There are three smaller cuts of salmon taken from the side of the fish. These are the most common cuts found at grocery most grocery stores.

1. LOIN: A larger, thicker cut from the top-middle of the fillet

2. BELLY: Comes from the thin, tapered belly side of the fillet and has a higher fat content

3. TAIL: The smallest and thinnest part of the fillet taken from the tail end of the side, just before the adipose fin all the way to the end where the tail was

ADDITIONAL CUTS

CENTER-CUT PORTION: This generally refers to a salmon portion from the premium part of the fillet, including the thicker part of the loin and a portion of the belly flap.

STEAKS: This is a cross-sectional cut of a salmon, perpendicular to the spine. It includes a section of the backbone, and sometimes even the belly cavity. It's shaped like a round steak, hence the name. These are best for grilling, broiling, and pan-searing. Steaks that are 1½ inches thick handle better, are easier to cook, and are more forgiving when preparing. If the steaks are too thin, they tend to break apart when transferring from the grill to a plate.

When cooking larger steaks, you can split the steak after cooking and serve half a steak per person. One final note: Steaks contain all bones including the backbone and pinbones. Be extremely careful when serving steaks and watch for bones as you eat.

STORING YOUR SALMON FOR PEAK FRESHNESS

Proper storage of fresh and frozen salmon is paramount to preserving quality. The key principle is temperature: Whether fresh or frozen, keep the fish at the right temperature. For fresh salmon, 32°F is ideal.

Your home refrigerator is probably warmer than 32°F, so you will want to take steps to keep your fish chilled. If it is wrapped in paper, remove the salmon; this paper can absorb moisture and isn't ideal for storage. Gently pat the fish dry with paper towels. This removes surface moisture, which helps preserve texture. Next, wrap the salmon tightly in plastic wrap, pressing out any air. Place the salmon in an airtight container. I have a small plastic storage container with a tight lid just for our salmon. Store it in the coldest part of your refrigerator—usually the back of the bottom shelf. For optimal storage, place a small frozen gel pack sealed in a zip-top bag on the salmon fillet before you close the container. This creates a microclimate closer to that ideal 32°F temperature. Remember, fresh salmon is highly perishable; plan to cook it within 1 to 3 days of purchase. If the salmon is vacuum-sealed, keep it in its packaging.

If you need to store salmon longer, freezing is the way to go. For the best quality, freeze your salmon quickly and keep it frozen solid at 0°F or below. Vacuum sealing before freezing is the gold standard, as it removes nearly all air. Alternatively, wrap the portion tightly in plastic wrap followed by a layer of heavy-duty aluminum foil, or place in a freezer-safe bag, squeezing out all excess air. Properly frozen salmon maintains good quality for up to 3 months.

THAWING SALMON SAFELY TO PRESERVE QUALITY

Thawing is just as critical as storing. Improper thawing can ruin the salmon's delicate texture and, more importantly, create food safety risks. The undisputed best and safest method is to thaw it slowly in the refrigerator. Simply move the frozen, still-wrapped salmon from the freezer to the refrigerator the day before you plan to cook it. Place it on a plate or in a shallow dish to catch any condensation or drips. This gradual thawing minimizes moisture loss and keeps the fish out of the temperature "danger zone," between 40°F and 140°F, where bacteria multiply rapidly.

If you're short on time, cold-water thawing is an acceptable, faster alternative, but only if the salmon is in completely airtight packaging (like a vacuum-sealed bag or a leak-proof freezer bag). Submerge the packaged salmon entirely in a bowl of cold tap water. Crucially, you must change the water every 30 minutes to ensure it stays cold. Depending on the thickness, it will thaw enough to cook in 30 to 45 minutes.

You should not thaw salmon at room temperature on the counter or use a microwave's defrost setting. Leaving fish out at room temperature allows harmful bacteria to proliferate quickly. Microwave thawing often begins to cook the thinner edges of the fish while the center remains frozen, resulting in an unevenly cooked, texturally compromised final product. Stick to refrigerator or cold-water thawing for the safest, most delicious results.

HANDLING THE BONES

Most of the salmon you buy aside from steaks are boneless. Fillets and portions do contain pinbones from time to time. These are easy to detect with your finger. Simply place the salmon on a cutting board (skin side down) and run your finger along the center of the surface of the fillet and feel for them. The pinbones start at the head end of the fillet and run halfway to the tail along the center. They are perpendicular to the flesh and were formerly attached to the spine. You can remove these using a set of fish tweezers or needle-nose pliers. Simply clamp on to the protruding tip of the bone and gently pull directly upward. The bone will offer a bit of resistance and then pop out leaving a small hole behind. Don't worry about the hole; it will seal up as the fish cooks. You can also more easily remove the pinbones after cooking, but be careful not to miss any. After the fish is cooked, the bones slide out without any resistance at all. I always remove all bones before cooking just to be safe.

SKIN VERSUS NO SKIN

I'm a huge fan of salmon skin and, when handled correctly, feel it dramatically improves the taste and texture of a finished dish. Salmon skin is loaded with nutrients and higher in omega-3s than the flesh. However, some people prefer a milder-tasting finished product, so use your judgment when it comes to keeping or ditching the skin.

Here's a basic rule: skin on for dry cooking methods; skin off for moist cooking methods. If you keep the skin on, make sure it is seasoned and crispy when served. No one likes flimsy and limp salmon skin. Removing skin is easiest when the fillet is whole.

COOKING TEMPERATURES & PROPER DONENESS

Salmon is finicky and requires precision when it comes to temperature and doneness. My recommendation for doneness is always medium, with a moist and pink center. Using this as a guide, the ideal temperature to achieve medium doneness varies slightly for each salmon species—for wild salmon it's 122°F and for farmed 124°F. Keep in mind that this temperature range doesn't square up with what food-safety experts suggest.

According to the FDA, fish like salmon should be cooked to an internal temperature of 145°F. This temperature is considered the minimum necessary to reduce the risk of foodborne illness and to kill harmful bacteria, but any fish cooked to this temperature will be more than "well done." Salmon cooked to 145°F will be firm, dry, and far less palatable. Cooking salmon to a lower temperature does come with some risk, but the risks can be reduced through careful purchase, handling, and preparation.

I've tested and cooked all types of species, forms, and cuts to determine the ideal cook temperature (based on preference). Full disclosure: I love salmon that is just barely cooked in the center, when it is still juicy and succulent but flakes when cut. For me, this is the ideal sensory pleasure.

Wild salmon has a different muscle structure and is leaner than farmed salmon, so it should be cooked to a lower temperature; farmed is far more fatty and has a more tender flesh, so it can be cooked to a slightly higher temperature. The key rule of thumb: Don't overcook your expensive wild salmon. Keep an eye on it like a killer whale while it cooks. Pull it from the heat right when it turns past 122°F in the middle. Let it rest for a few minutes and enjoy. Farmed salmon is more forgiving. You can bring it up to a higher internal temperature and it will keep its desirable qualities. It doesn't require as much attention, though you don't want to allow the internal temperature to move past 124°F before pulling it from the heat. It also goes without saying: Get yourself a really good instant-read digital thermometer and use it.

FOR WILD SALMON

The ideal cook temperature is 122°F.

RARE (110°F): Rare (mostly raw) salmon will have slightly translucent flesh and will be soft and raw in the center—similar to the tataki recipe on page 201.

MEDIUM-RARE (120 TO 122°F): Salmon cooked medium-rare will be firm on the outside and slightly opaque, with a barely raw and succulent center. It's also deliciously moist throughout. This is the preferred doneness for wild salmon.

MEDIUM (125 TO 130°F): Medium-cooked salmon is firmer to the touch and has a pink and moist center that is no longer rare.

MEDIUM-WELL (135 TO 140°F): Salmon cooked medium-well is firmer, with a lighter, slightly dry center.

WELL-DONE (145°F OR ABOVE): The salmon is now quite firm with no pink color left in the center. It is dry and flaky.

FOR FARMED SALMON

The ideal cook temperature is 124°F.

RARE (115°F): Rare (mostly raw) salmon will have translucent flesh and will be soft and silky-smooth in the center—similar to the tataki recipe on page 201.

MEDIUM-RARE (124 TO 126°F): Medium-rare salmon will turn slightly opaque with a soft texture. It's also deliciously moist throughout. This is my preferred doneness for farmed salmon.

MEDIUM (130 TO 135°F): Salmon cooled until medium is fully opaque. It is firmer to the touch and has a slightly pink center.

MEDIUM-WELL (135 TO 140°F): Medium-well salmon is firmer yet with a lighter pink center when cooked. It's also less moist compared to medium salmon.

WELL-DONE (145°F OR ABOVE): The salmon is now quite firm with no pink color left in the center.

NOTE: The USDA recommends avoiding consumption of raw or rare (undercooked) fish, including salmon, and suggests a minimum cook temperature of 145°F. If you do consume undercooked fish, make sure it is sashimi-grade, previously deep-frozen, to reduce bacterial risk.

PRE-SALT BEFORE YOU COOK

Chefs are always trying to find a better, more efficient way to increase deliciousness. Lightly salting fish before cooking is one of those methods. I use it all the time, and it always makes the end result better. I use it for almost every protein I cook as it works regardless of species. Keep in mind, pre-salting in this sense is different from seasoning with salt. Pre-salting is done to improve the protein prior to cooking and serving. Salting to season is done during and at the end of cooking to perfect flavor and balance.

There are many names for the method: salting, pre-salting, salt-curing, and short-curing. Or you can call it what it is: salting. Why is salting so beneficial? It all has to do with diffusion and osmosis. You can look into these two processes in more detail on your own. However, when it comes to salmon, the results are fantastic.

HOW SALTING, BRINING, OR SALT-CURING HELPS

IMPROVES FLAVOR: Salt, a salt-curing mix, or a brine infuses the salmon with flavor and helps to season it throughout.

REDUCES ALBUMIN PURGE: Albumin is the white stuff that sometimes oozes out of salmon when you cook it. Albumin is a protein that's trapped between the muscle fibers of the fish. When heated, these fibers contract and squeeze out the albumin. It's not harmful, nor does it impact flavor, but it's not the most appetizing thing to look at. You can always remove it with a spoon before serving. Salting, whether dry or in a wet brine, helps to break down some of these muscle fibers. This means they won't tighten as much when cooked, and less albumin gets pushed out. The result is a cleaner, better-looking product.

REDUCES PAN SPLATTER: Salting draws out moisture, which, in turn, reduces water purge and splatter during cooking. Salted portions cook with less mess and perform better in the pan. They tend not to stick for the same reason—there's less water purging into the pan, disrupting the cooking process, and causing the surface of the fish to stick.

IMPROVES TEXTURE: Salting can help to firm up the texture of the fish, making it juicier. The salt causes the fish to lose water while also binding some of the water that is left within the muscle, so the end result is moist and succulent. That's a win-win.

IMPROVES PRESERVATION: The salt acts as a preservative due to the reduction of available water in the fillet, inhibiting bacterial growth and extending shelf life.

TYPES OF BRINES AND CURES

WET BRINE: The salmon is submerged in a liquid solution of salt, sugar, and water. The preferred ratio of salt and sugar in a wet brine is 1½ percent salt and 1½ percent sugar by weight of the salmon being cured. Note that the measure doesn't have to be perfect.

DRY-CURING: The salmon is covered with a dry mixture of salt, sugar, and sometimes other seasonings. For a 2-pound side of salmon, use 2 tablespoons kosher salt and 2 tablespoons organic granulated sugar spread evenly over the fillet and cure for at least 24 hours in the refrigerator.

FOR SMOKED & CURED SALMON

COLD SMOKE AND HOT SMOKE

COLD-SMOKED SALMON is kept at 90°F or lower while in the smokehouse, a temperature that is cool enough to avoid denaturing the proteins of the fish but warm enough to infuse delicious flavor. Fillets are held at this temperature for between 8 to 10 hours before being set aside to cool and rest before slicing and packaging.

HOT-SMOKED SALMON is processed at 160°F or higher, smoking the fish until it reaches an internal temperature of 145°F before cooling, processing, and packaging. It usually takes 1½ to 2 hours to properly hot-smoke a side of salmon.

CURED SALMON: GRAVLAX & LOX

GRAVLAX is a Nordic delicacy of cured salmon in which the fish is "buried" ("grav" in Swedish) in a mixture of salt, sugar, and dill. This dry cure draws out moisture, firming the flesh and infusing it with flavor. Unlike smoked salmon, gravlax is not smoked, resulting in a fresh, clean taste and a silky texture. It's typically served thinly sliced, often with mustard sauce and dark bread.

LOX is a fillet of salmon that has been cured exclusively in salt or a salt-sugar mixture. It's not smoked, unlike many other preparations of salmon. This curing process gives lox its characteristically smooth, silky texture and a salty, rich flavor. Traditionally, lox was made from the belly of the salmon, but today other parts of the fish may be used. It's often served on bagels with cream cheese, tomatoes, onions, and capers, and is a staple of Jewish delicatessens.

COLD-SMOKED SALMON: NOVA & SCOTTISH SMOKED

NOVA SMOKED SALMON, OFTEN CALLED "NOVA LOX," is a type of cold-smoked salmon that originates in Nova Scotia, Canada. It's made by curing salmon fillets in a mixture of salt and sugar, then cold-smoking them at low temperatures. This process results in a silky-smooth texture and a delicate smoky flavor. Nova is typically sliced very thin and is often enjoyed on bagels with cream cheese or in appetizers and canapés. It's known for a subtle smoky flavor that doesn't overpower the natural taste of the salmon.

SCOTTISH SMOKED SALMON is renowned for its distinctive flavor and texture, often attributed to traditional smoking methods and the unique environment of Scotland. It's typically cured with salt and sometimes sugar, then cold-smoked using wood from native Scottish trees like oak and beech; sometimes whisky-barrel wood is used. This imparts a rich, smoky flavor with a subtle sweetness. The texture is delicate and melts in your mouth, with a beautiful translucent orange color. Scottish smoked salmon is often considered a premium product, prized for its quality and craftsmanship.

HOT-SMOKED SALMON: CANDY & KIPPERED

CANDY-SMOKED SALMON is a sweet and savory treat made by curing salmon in a mixture of salt and brown sugar, then hot-smoking it until it develops a firm, almost jerky-like texture, and a caramelized candy-like crust. This process results in a concentrated flavor that's both smoky and sweet with a chewy texture. It can be flaked and added to salads, pasta dishes, or appetizers.

KIPPERED/HOT-SMOKED SALMON is fully cooked during the smoking process and at a higher temperature (around 180°F) than cold-smoked varieties. This gives it a firm, flaky texture, and a more intense smoky flavor. Before smoking, the salmon is typically brined in a mixture of salt, sugar, and sometimes other seasonings. This brine serves to infuse the fish with flavor, preserve it, and help it retain moisture during the hot-smoking process. Kippered salmon is a ready-to-eat product and can be flaked into salads or used in a variety of recipes.

COOKING METHODS

What happens when we cook salmon? The key is knowing how protein reacts when heated. Proteins in their natural state have a three-dimensional structure that is important to their function, which is to provide the necessary amino acids for building and repairing the muscle tissue crucial for the fish's movement. When salmon is cooked, we manipulate the bonds within the protein, through the application of heat, acid, or salt, to alter the composition of the flesh. This alteration is also called denaturing, a word that describes the unwinding of the protein structure.

A protein becomes denatured when the bonds that hold the amino acids together are broken due to heat. As proteins cook (denature) and unwind they coagulate (stick together) and become insoluble in water. The act of cooking is nothing more than a controlled process of unwinding amino acids and proteins to a desired doneness or end result.

What about all that water? The unfolding of a protein as it cooks weakens its ability to hold water molecules, causing some water to be expelled. This is why salmon splatters and steams when you place it in a hot pan. And that white stuff that appears on the fillet as it cooks? It's albumin, mentioned earlier, and it is fine to eat.

Cooking also causes the proteins to become firmer and less translucent. Salmon will shift from flimsy to firm and flaky. The longer you subject the fish to heat, the firmer and drier it will get. Cook it too long and it will be completely firm and dry. High-heat cooking methods and longer cook times will also lead to greater water loss and drier texture.

Understanding how this transformation works and learning how to control it allows for vast improvements in the overall cooking experience and end results. By considering the interplay of these reactions, cooks can optimize the process and create consistent and delicious results.

DRY-HEAT COOKING

These cooking techniques use hot air or conduction with fat to transfer heat to food without the presence of any moisture (water, broth, or liquid). There are multiple benefits of dry-heat cooking:

FLAVOR AND TEXTURE: Dry-heat cooking often produces rich flavors and textures like crispy skin on salmon.

BROWNING AND CARAMELIZATION: Add depth and flavor.

VERSATILITY: Dry heat can be applied in many ways, leading to a wide range of cooking methods—from using the stovetop in a cast-iron skillet to using a toaster oven or an air fryer.

SIMPLICITY: Many dry-heat cooking methods require minimal equipment and are easy to master.

Some common dry-heat cooking methods are:

PAN-SEARING: Cooking food at high heat in a minimal amount of fat until browned.

SAUTÉING: Quickly cooking food in a pan over medium-high heat with a small amount of fat.

PAN-FRYING: Cooking food in a pan with a moderate amount of fat.

ROASTING: Cooking food in an oven with a high, dry heat to brown, then a lower heat to finish.

BAKING: Similar to roasting, using dry heat but at a constant temperature.

GRILLING: Cooking food over direct heat from below, often on a grill grate.

BROILING: Cooking food under direct heat from above in an oven.

AIR-FRYING: Cooking food under direct, dry circulating heat in a closed container.

MOIST-HEAT COOKING

Moist-heat cooking methods involve using liquid, like water, broth, or wine, or steam to transfer heat to food. They are excellent for tenderizing and adding moisture to foods that might otherwise dry out. What makes them special?

TENDERIZING: Moist-heat cooking methods often run at higher temperatures and also help make muscle and connective tissues incredibly tender and succulent.

INFUSING FLAVOR: The cooking liquid becomes infused with the flavors of the food and any added aromatics, creating a delicious sauce or gravy.

MAINTAINING MOISTURE: Moist-heat cooking helps to keep food from drying out, resulting in juicy and flavorful dishes.

VERSATILITY: You can use moist heat to cook a wide variety of foods.

COMMON MOIST-HEAT COOKING METHODS USED FOR SEAFOOD INCLUDE:

SIMMERING: Cooking food in liquid that is just below the boiling point.

POACHING: Gently cooking food in liquid that is barely simmering.

STEAMING: Cooking food with the steam from boiling water.

COOKING SALMON AT HOME

TOOL & EQUIPMENT RECOMMENDATIONS

BAKING SHEET (STAINLESS STEEL): 7 x 9 x 1-inch

BLENDER

CAST-IRON SKILLET (12-INCH PRE-SEASONED): This is an essential kitchen favorite and, if maintained correctly, eliminates the need for a nonstick pan. Cast-iron works on all types of range tops, including induction.

CHEF'S KNIFE: A high-quality 7- to 9-inch chef's knife that is made from high-carbon steel. Purchase a chef's knife plus a 9-inch slicing knife for precision cutting of raw salmon. Note that knives go from affordable to super expensive.

FINE-MESH SIEVE

FISH-BONE TWEEZERS: Just in case the fish you buy has bones. Choose stainless steel or purchase inexpensive needle-nose pliers at a hardware store, but don't put the pliers in the dishwasher after use; wash and dry by hand, then spray with oil to keep from rusting.

FISH SPATULA: Choose stainless steel. I use mine all the time and like the way it feels when working with fish.

INSTANT-READ DIGITAL THERMOMETER: Of all the tools, this is probably the most important if proper doneness is your goal.

MASON JARS

MICROPLANE GRATER

MICROWAVE-SAFE BOWL

MINI MELON BALLER

PEPPER MILL

POT (6-QUART)

ROASTING FORK

ROASTING PLANKS

SLICING KNIFE: A high-quality straight-edge knife for cutting fillets and sashimi.

SMALL FOOD PROCESSOR

SMALL MANDOLINE (PLASTIC WITH STEEL BLADE)

STAINLESS STEEL RING MOLD

STAINLESS STEEL SKEWERS

STAINLESS STEEL SKILLET (14-INCH HEAVY-GAUGE): It should be 3 to 4 inches deep with a lid.

TONGS

VEGETABLE PEELER

WOODEN SKEWERS

ZESTER

THE SALMON PANTRY

Aluminum foil

Balsamic vinegar

Cooking spray

Diamond Crystal kosher salt

Dijon mustard

Dried dill

Dried ginger powder

Dried thyme

Good-quality olive oil

Granulated garlic

Honey

Maldon flaky sea salt

Maple sugar

Maple syrup

Onion powder

Parchment paper

Plastic wrap

Rice vinegar

Smoked paprika

Tamari

Togarashi

Whole black peppercorns

OPPOSITE: Additional pantry items, including fish sauce, sesame oil, toasted sesame seeds, Japanese barbecue sauce, fleur de sel, miso, coconut milk, pickled ginger, Merkén pepper, sansho pepper, fennel pollen, red curry paste, garbanzo beans, mayonnaise, and Japanese shichimi togarashi.

ENDNOTES

Page 27: "The very first hatchery . . ." John R. Moring, "The Creation of the First Public Salmon Hatchery in the United States." *Fisheries*, vol. 25, issue 7, July 2000, 6–12.

Page 27: "Just twenty years later, in 1891 . . ." Terry Ellison, "Development of Public and Private Hatcheries in Alaska." Report presented at the Aquaculture Association of Canada, Vancouver, British Columbia, June 1–3, 1992, Alaska Resources Library & Information Services (ARLIS).

Page 27: "By most measures, the plan . . ." Alaska Salmon Hatcheries Contributing to Fisheries and Sustainability PNP Hatchery Program, Alaska Department of Fish and Game—Division of Commercial Fisheries, Juneau, Alaska, website.

Page 29: "The farming of fish is an ancient practice . . ." Tsuneo Nakajima, Mark J. Hudson, Junzo Uchiyama, Keisuke Makibayashi, and Juzhong Zhang, "Common Carp Aquaculture in Neolithic China Dates Back 8,000 Years." *Nature Ecology & Evolution* 3, 1415–1418, September 2019.

Page 29: "The U.S. National Oceanographic and Atmospheric Administration defines aquaculture . . . "What is Aquaculture?" National Ocean and Atmospheric Administration (NOAA), official website of the United States government.

Page 30: "Our current form of domesticated salmon originates in Norway . . ." Colin Nash: *The History of Aquaculture* (Hoboken, New Jersey: Wiley-Blackwell, 2011), 121.

Page 30: "The Norwegians formalized regulation in the Aquaculture Act of 1981." Norwegian Aquaculture Act of 2006.

Page 30: "In the mid-1980s, Scotland, Chile, and Canada were seeded . . ." B. Aarseth and S. E. Jakobsen. "On a Clear Day You Can See All the Way to Brussels: The Transformations of Aquaculture Regulation in Norway," SNF Working Paper, no. 63/04 (Bergen, Norway: Institute for Research in Economics and Business Administration, 2004).

Page 30: "By February of 1990, the U.S. Department of Commerce . . ." United States—Imposition of Anti-dumping Duties on Imports of Fresh and Chilled Atlantic Salmon from Norway, Report of the Panel adopted by the Committee on Anti-Dumping Practices, April 27, 1994 (ADP/87). November 30, 1992, 27.

Page 30: "Unlike terrestrial farming, salmon aquaculture is inherently mobile. . . ." Marianne Elisabeth Lien, *Becoming Salmon: Aquaculture and the Domestication of a Fish* (Oakland, California: University of California Press, 2015), 29.

Part 2

SALMON RECIPES

BAKING

Baking is a dry-heat cooking method where you cook fish in an oven at a constant temperature. It's a healthy and easy way to prepare fish, as it requires little to no added fat. Baking temperatures for fish usually range from 350°F to 450°F, depending on the thickness of the fish and the desired result. I tend toward the 350°F range for most salmon preparations. Fish can be baked uncovered on a baking sheet lined with foil—with or without a rack. Baking is great for fish—you can bake whole fish, fillets, or steaks. It is also so easy—once the fish is in the oven, you can leave it alone until it's cooked. This frees you up to prepare other parts of your meal.

HERE ARE SOME BASIC TIPS FOR BAKING:

DRY THE FISH: Pat the salmon dry with paper towels before seasoning and cooking to increase the potential for browning.

SEASON THE FISH: At a minimum, use good-quality salt and pepper. If you have time, lightly cure the fish with salt (or a salt and sugar combination) and refrigerate for 30 minutes.

USE THE RIGHT RACK: When baking salmon, it is best to use the middle rack to assure even temperature.

USE THE RIGHT SETTING: Some ovens have a convection setting; unless instructed otherwise, cook without convection.

DON'T PEEK: Once the fish is in the oven, don't open the oven door again until it's time to check for doneness.

DON'T OVERCOOK: Salmon cooks quickly, so keep an eye on it. Insert an instant-read digital thermometer in the thickest part of the fillet and take a reading to determine if the fish is cooked (122°F for wild, 124°F for farmed). The thickest part of the salmon will be opaque and flake easily with a fork.

LET THE FISH REST: Once the desired temperature is reached, remove the salmon from the oven and let it rest for a few minutes on a plate, skin side up if the fillet has skin.

USE THE RIGHT TOOL: Transfer the fish to a plate using a fish spatula or a metal spatula that is large enough to lift the fish without it breaking.

OPPOSITE: The Domeyko Fish Farm located on the southwest shore of Lake Llanquihue in Los Lagos, Chile.

BAKED
SALMON QUICHE
WITH
ONIONS & A SMOKED SALMON TOPPER

Members of my family are gluten- and dairy-free, so this recipe eliminates both and it's still delicious. I use a gluten-free Trader Joe's piecrust and replace dairy with almond milk (we make our own, but you can use store-bought). The rest of the recipe is made from scratch. Rest this quiche overnight in the refrigerator and then reheat it for 90 seconds in a microwave oven set to medium (number 7). It is fantastic. You could also drizzle the smoked salmon garnish with ponzu and spicy mayo for a kick of added deliciousness.

SERVES 4

3 tablespoons extra-virgin olive oil

1 medium shallot, julienned

1 small white onion, julienned

4 scallions, thinly sliced

Kosher salt and freshly ground black pepper

1 bunch spinach

One 9-inch premade piecrust

3 large eggs

2 cups almond milk

12 ounces cured salmon, thinly sliced (see recipe, page 102)

4 ounces smoked Nova salmon, thinly sliced, and arugula sprouts for serving (optional)

1. Preheat the oven to 325°F.

2. In a medium sauté pan, heat 2 tablespoons of the olive oil over medium heat until hot, then add the shallot, onion, and scallions. Cover and cook until wilted, 4 to 5 minutes. Remove the lid and continue to cook until all moisture has evaporated. Transfer the onion mixture to a bowl and season with salt and pepper. Set aside.

3. Return the pan to medium heat and add the remaining 1 tablespoon olive oil. Add the spinach and sauté until wilted and dry, 3 to 4 minutes. Transfer the spinach to the bowl with the onion mixture and stir to combine.

4. Place the piecrust on a baking sheet. Parbake in the oven until it is dry and firm to the touch but not brown, about 8 minutes. Remove from the oven and allow to cool on the baking sheet.

5. In a medium bowl, whisk together the eggs and almond milk.

6. Keeping the piecrust on the baking sheet, spread a shallow layer of onions and spinach on the bottom of the crust. Add a layer of cured salmon, then repeat with another layer of the onion-spinach mixture. Pour ¼ cup of the egg mixture over the top and then repeat the process several times layering salmon, then the onion-spinach mixture and another ¼ cup of the egg mixture, until the piecrust is filled. Pour any excess egg mixture evenly over the top. Gently tap the piecrust to assure the egg mixture has settled.

7. Bake the quiche for 18 to 20 minutes, until a toothpick can be inserted and removed from the center without any moisture. The internal temperature should be 145°F on an instant-read thermometer.

8. Allow the quiche to cool, then refrigerate overnight. Portion into 8 slices and microwave until warmed through. Top with the Nova salmon and arugula sprouts, if using, and serve.

BAKED SALMON WITH POLENTA & BRAISED FENNEL

Polenta is fabulous and easy to prepare, and I encourage more home cooks to try it. It's just cornmeal and liquid cooked until reconstituted, and you can find good-quality cornmeal at most supermarkets. If you are highly committed like me, an amazing option is to purchase late-season fresh sweet corn at your local farmers market and make your own cornmeal by shaving off the kernels and drying them in a dehydrator before processing into meal in a dedicated burr grinder (typically used for coffee beans). My homemade late-season sweet cornmeal makes the best polenta and reminds me of summer during winter meals.

SERVES 4 ✻ COOK TO 122°F FOR WILD, 124°F FOR FARMED, OR TO DESIRED DONENESS

One 1-pound skinless, boneless salmon fillet, cut into 4 portions

2 teaspoons sea salt, plus more to taste

2 teaspoons freshly ground black pepper, plus more to taste

¼ cup extra-virgin olive oil, plus more for drizzling

½ cup organic dry polenta cornmeal (preferably Bob's Red Mill)

2 cups low-sodium chicken broth or water, plus more as needed

1 bulb fennel, cored and thinly sliced

1 medium shallot, julienned

¼ cup dry white wine

1 fresh shaved fennel bulb, 1 sautéed shallot, mustard greens, red Russian kale, and fennel fronds for garnish (optional)

1. Preheat the oven to 375°F.

2. Place the salmon on a baking sheet lined with foil. Season the salmon with 2 teaspoons salt and pepper and drizzle with olive oil; set aside.

3. Place 2 tablespoons of the olive oil in a medium saucepan set over medium heat. Add the cornmeal and lightly toast, stirring occasionally. Add the broth and bring to a simmer. Allow to simmer 12 to 15 minutes, stirring occasionally, until the broth is absorbed. Turn the heat off and cover. Let it rest on the stovetop for another 5 minutes. The moisture will continue to absorb.

4. In a medium sauté pan, add the remaining 2 tablespoons olive oil and warm over medium heat. Add the fennel and stir. Sauté for 1 to 2 minutes, until slightly softened. Add the shallot, sauté for another 1 to 2 minutes, then add the wine and cook until the fennel is tender and lightly braised, about 10 minutes. Taste and season with salt and pepper as needed.

5. Meanwhile, bake the salmon for about 10 minutes, until an instant-read thermometer inserted into the thickest part of a fillet is 122°F for wild, 124°F for farmed, or the fish is cooked to desired doneness. Rest the salmon on a plate for 3 to 4 minutes.

6. To serve, check the polenta for texture. If too thick, place it over low heat and stir in a bit more broth or water until creamy and smooth. Spoon polenta onto each of four serving plates. Place the braised fennel next to the polenta and top with a salmon portion. If desired, garnish with a small salad.

BAKED SALMON WITH APPLE-WALNUT SALAD

During autumn, our local CSA offers seven different varieties of apples, and I've tried them all. My favorite apple for this recipe is a fresh-picked Honeycrisp—for the flavor and texture. Salmon marries well with the bright flavor of Honeycrisp apples and toasted walnuts. However, you can substitute any kind of apple and nut you prefer. I've made this with Granny Smiths (also Red Delicious) and toasted hazelnuts, too.

SERVES 4 ✻ COOK TO 122°F FOR WILD, 124°F FOR FARMED, OR TO DESIRED DONENESS

1 teaspoon kosher salt, plus more to taste

½ teaspoon fresh thyme leaves

1 pinch paprika

Four 3-ounce skinless, boneless salmon fillets

½ cup walnut halves

½ cup extra-virgin olive oil, plus more for coating

1 tablespoon Dijon mustard

¼ cup balsamic vinegar

1 tablespoon roasted shallot (see Note)

¼ cup thinly shaved red onion

1 tablespoon tarragon leaves, coarsely chopped, plus 1 tablespoon leaves for garnish

1 tablespoon dried cranberries, chopped

1 Honeycrisp apple, cored and cut into ½-inch chunks

1 medium cucumber, peeled and cut into ½-inch chunks

Freshly ground black pepper to taste

4 cups (about 2 ounces) baby salad greens (spring greens, kale, chard)

1. Combine the 1 teaspoon salt, thyme, and paprika in a small bowl. Place the salmon on a plate and sprinkle with the salt mixture. Refrigerate, covered, for up to 1 hour.

2. Preheat the oven to 350°F.

3. Spread the walnuts out on a baking sheet in a single layer. Bake for 6 to 8 minutes until lightly toasted and golden brown. Transfer the walnuts to a bowl to cool, then coarsely chop.

4. Place the salmon fillets on a foil-lined baking sheet coated with olive oil and bake for 8 to 10 minutes, until an instant-read thermometer inserted into the thickest part of a fillet is 122°F for wild, 124°F for farmed, or the fish is cooked to desired doneness. Cool to room temperature.

5. To prepare the dressing, place the Dijon mustard in a large bowl. Whisk the olive oil into the mustard in a steady stream. Continue whisking until the oil is fully incorporated and an emulsion forms. (An emulsion is when liquids that don't naturally mix, like oil and water, come together and stay that way. Mustard is the binder, and the gentle whisking is what allows the process to occur.) Whisk in the vinegar in a steady stream until incorporated. To the bowl of dressing, add three-quarters of the walnuts along with the shallot, onion, tarragon, cranberries, apple, and cucumber. Toss with a spoon until coated. Season with salt and pepper.

6. To serve, portion one cup of baby greens and approximately ½ cup of the apple mixture into each of four plates. Top with a portion of the salmon, then sprinkle with the remaining toasted walnuts. Garnish with tarragon leaves and serve.

Note: To prepare the roasted shallot, simply peel and halve a medium shallot, place in a glass bowl, add two tablespoons olive oil, and microwave for 45 to 60 seconds. Crush with a fork and you are good to go.

BAKED

SALMON BLT ON HEARTY WHOLE GRAIN BREAD

Aside from smoked variations, salmon does not appear in many sandwiches. However, salmon competes directly with tuna as a wonderful choice. For this recipe, rather than flake and blend with mayonnaise like tuna, I bake thin slices of seasoned salmon loin and use it to make a delicious BLT. And yes—I still use bacon. Nueske's wild cherrywood smoked uncured bacon works best with salmon, but you can use any bacon you like.

SERVES 4 ✳ COOK TO 122°F FOR WILD, 124°F FOR FARMED, OR TO DESIRED DONENESS

- **1 tablespoon extra-virgin olive oil**
- **One 1-pound skinless, boneless salmon loin, cut into ¼-inch-thick slices**
- **1 teaspoon sea salt**
- **½ teaspoon freshly ground black pepper**
- **2 to 3 tablespoons mayonnaise**
- **8 slices bread**
- **8 strips cooked bacon, cut in half, at room temperature**
- **4 leaves Bibb lettuce**
- **8 thin slices tomato (about 2 medium)**

1. Preheat the oven to 300°F.

2. Line a baking sheet with foil and coat with the olive oil. Place the salmon on the baking sheet and season with the salt and pepper. Bake the salmon 2 to 3 minutes, until an instant-read thermometer inserted into the thickest part of a fillet is 122°F for wild, 124°F for farmed, or the fish is cooked to desired doneness. Cool to room temperature, then break into large chunks.

3. Lightly spread the mayonnaise on each slice of bread. Build a sandwich by layering a piece of bread with 4 bacon strip halves, 1 lettuce leaf, 2 tomato slices, and slices of salmon. Top with another piece of bread. Secure the sandwiches with toothpicks. Repeat to create 3 more sandwiches. Serve with a side of dressed green salad if you like.

BAKED SALMON WITH COCONUT SWEET POTATO RED CURRY

As you will see in this book, my recipes are globally informed. This recipe leans heavily on the flavor profiles and techniques of Southeast Asia and India—places where salmon consumption is uncommon but where deliciousness is plentiful. For this recipe, I replaced shrimp with salmon and adjusted to optimize flavor. The result is fantastic.

SERVES 4 ✻ COOK TO 122°F FOR WILD, 124°F FOR FARMED, OR TO DESIRED DONENESS

- Four 4-ounce skin-on, boneless center-cut salmon fillets
- 6 tablespoons extra-virgin olive oil, plus more for coating
- Sea salt and freshly ground black pepper
- ¼ cup diced white onion
- ¼ cup diced red bell pepper
- 2 tablespoons diced celery
- 2 cloves garlic, minced
- One 1-inch knob fresh ginger, grated
- 1 sweet potato, peeled and diced
- 1 Yukon gold potato, peeled and diced
- One 13-ounce can unsweetened coconut milk (preferably Native Forest Organic, BPA free)
- 1½ cups low-sodium chicken broth or water
- ¼ cup maple syrup, plus more to taste
- 2 tablespoons red curry paste (preferably Thai Kitchen), plus more to taste
- 2 cups cooked basmati or brown rice, warmed through
- 2 tablespoons chopped cilantro
- 1 teaspoon fresh basil blossoms (optional)

1. Preheat the oven to 350°F.

2. Place the salmon on a foil-lined baking sheet coated with olive oil and season with salt and pepper. Brush the tops with 2 tablespoons of the olive oil and set aside.

3. In a large pot, heat 2 tablespoons olive oil over medium heat. Add the onion, bell pepper, and celery and sauté until just tender, 3 to 4 minutes. Add the garlic and ginger and sauté until tender, 1 to 2 minutes.

4. Add the potatoes, coconut milk, and broth and stir. Bring to a simmer. Add the maple syrup and red curry paste and simmer for 10 minutes. Adjust the seasonings, adding salt, pepper, and more maple syrup and curry paste, if needed. Keep warm on low heat while you prepare the salmon.

5. In a large cast-iron skillet, heat the remaining 2 tablespoons olive oil over medium heat. Add the salmon fillets, skin side down, and sear until the edges of the skin begin to brown, 2 to 3 minutes. Transfer the portions, skin side up, to another baking sheet covered with foil and coated with olive oil. Bake 6 to 8 minutes, until an instant-read thermometer inserted into the thickest part of a fillet is 122°F for wild, 124°F for farmed, or the fish is cooked to desired doneness. Rest the salmon on a plate, skin side up, for a few minutes.

6. To serve, place a scoop of rice on one side of each of four serving bowls. Ladle the coconut sweet potato curry next to the rice. Sprinkle with cilantro. Top each portion with a salmon fillet, garnish with fresh basil blossoms, if using, and serve.

BAKED

SALMON & MUSSEL PAELLA

Saffron-scented rice meets the sea in this vibrant paella. Flaky salmon and plump mussels mingle with sweet peppers, fennel, and olives, creating a savory burst of flavors. With practice, you can turn this into a one-pot meal. Double the recipe and you'll have enough for a second delicious meal the next day.

SERVES 4

One 12-ounce skinless, boneless salmon fillet, cut into ½-inch pieces

Kosher salt and freshly ground black pepper

½ teaspoon paprika

⅓ cup extra-virgin olive oil

¼ cup diced white onion

2 tablespoons minced garlic

½ fennel bulb, trimmed and cut into ½-inch wedges

¼ cup diced roasted red bell pepper

¼ cup Manzanilla olives, halved

1½ cups Bomba rice (or short-grain rice)

2½ cups low-sodium chicken broth

½ cup dry white wine

½ teaspoon saffron threads

24 medium-size mussels, washed and debearded

1. Preheat the oven to 325°F.

2. In a medium bowl, season the salmon with salt, pepper, and paprika, and drizzle with 1 tablespoon of the olive oil. Toss to coat.

3. Pour the remaining olive oil into a large, heavy-bottomed pot or Dutch oven and set over medium heat. Sear the salmon for 2 to 3 minutes; the pieces will not be fully cooked. Transfer to a plate.

4. To the pot, add the onion, garlic, fennel, and bell pepper. Sauté until the fennel and onion start to become tender, 3 to 4 minutes. Stir in the olives.

5. Add the rice to the pot and stir until coated with olive oil; cook for 1 to 2 minutes. Add the broth, wine, and saffron and season with salt and pepper. Stir to combine. Cover and cook for 12 minutes, until the rice is tender; it won't be fully cooked.

6. Transfer the rice mixture to a paella pan. Line the edge of the pan with the mussels and scatter the salmon over the rice in the center of the pan. Bake in the oven for 7 to 9 minutes, or until the mussels have opened and the salmon is flaky. Serve from the pan.

BAKED

COULIBIAC OF SALMON

This recipe is probably the most advanced in the book, but don't be afraid. Take your time and be persistent. The end result is worth it, and I've done my best to simplify the recipe. Consider it a special occasion item.

SERVES 4 ✳ COOK TO 122°F FOR WILD, 124°F FOR FARMED, OR TO PREFERENCE

3 tablespoons unsalted butter

2 tablespoons minced shallot

2 tablespoons thinly sliced garlic

16 ounces button mushrooms, diced small

¾ cup Madeira

Kosher salt and freshly ground black pepper

⅔ cup jasmine rice

2 teaspoons thinly sliced chives

2 teaspoons finely chopped flat-leaf parsley leaves

One 10-ounce skinless, boneless salmon loin

1 sheet puff pastry, thawed

All-purpose flour for work surface

1 large egg, beaten

Maldon flaky sea salt

Cucumber & Yogurt Salad (recipe follows)

1. Warm a large sauté pan over medium heat and add the butter. Once melted, add the shallot and garlic and cook until softened, 3 to 4 minutes. Add the mushrooms and cook until all moisture has been released, about 10 minutes. Deglaze the pan with the Madeira and reduce until 80 percent of the liquid has evaporated. Season with salt and pepper and set aside until completely cool.

2. In a small saucepan, cook the rice according to package instructions. Once cooked, remove from the heat and allow to cool completely.

3. In a medium bowl, combine the cooked rice, mushroom mixture, chives, and parsley and mix thoroughly. Taste and season with salt and pepper as needed.

4. Measure out a piece of plastic wrap that is larger than the salmon loin.

5. Pour ⅔ cup of the rice and mushroom mixture onto the plastic wrap and use wet hands or a damp rolling pin to roll the mixture out until it's ⅛ inch thick and large enough to cover the entire salmon loin. Place the salmon loin along one side of the mixture. Use the plastic wrap to help flip the loin and mixture so that the mixture is completely coating the outside of the loin. Fold in the ends of the plastic wrap to wrap the loin tightly. Refrigerate for 2 hours.

6. Preheat the oven to 425°F.

7. Remove the salmon from the refrigerator. Lay the sheet of puff pastry on a lightly floured surface. Unwrap the rice-covered salmon loin and place it along one side of the puff pastry. Use the edge of the puff pastry to flip the salmon loin until it is completely covered by the pastry, over the top and along the sides. Trim off any excess edges of the puff pastry. Place the wrapped salmon seam side down on a baking sheet lined with parchment paper. Brush the top with the beaten egg and sprinkle with Maldon salt.

8. Bake the salmon coulibiac until the puff pastry is golden and an instant-read thermometer inserted into the salmon is 122°F for wild or 124°F for farmed, or the fish is cooked to desired doneness, 12 to 15 minutes. Once cooked through, allow it to rest for 8 to 10 minutes before slicing into it.

9. To serve, slice the coulibiac into 2-inch-thick slices and serve with the cucumber and yogurt salad.

CUCUMBER & YOGURT SALAD

MAKES 1 CUP

- 1 English cucumber, cut into matchsticks
- ¼ fennel bulb, thinly sliced
- ¼ red onion, thinly sliced
- ½ cup Greek yogurt
- 2 tablespoons extra-virgin olive oil
- 1 teaspoon finely chopped dill
- Zest of 1 lemon, finely grated
- 1 teaspoon freshly squeezed lemon juice
- Kosher salt and freshly ground black pepper

In a large bowl, combine the cucumber, fennel, onion, yogurt, olive oil, dill, lemon zest, and lemon juice. Stir gently. Season with salt and pepper.

BAKED SALMON GÜVEÇ WITH ZHOUG

Güveç are Turkish stews baked in clay dishes or pots, usually made with meat, poultry, or vegetables. In eastern Turkey and some Baltic countries, it is traditional for a cook to carry their güveç to the neighborhood bakery to finish in a hot stone oven. This is my interpretation using salmon and zhoug—a celebration of the delicious flavors of the Eastern Mediterranean inspired by one of my favorite chefs in New England, Ana Sortun, of Sofra Bakery and Oleana in Boston, Massachusetts.

You'll need four oven-safe ceramic bowls for baking and serving, if you want to be authentic.

SERVES 4 ✳ COOK TO 122°F FOR WILD, 124°F FOR FARMED, OR TO DESIRED DONENESS

Four 4-ounce skinless, boneless salmon fillets

Kosher salt and freshly ground black pepper

2 tablespoons extra-virgin olive oil

GÜVEÇ

¼ cup diced white onion

1 clove garlic, minced

½ cup diced butternut squash

One 15-ounce can cannellini beans, drained and rinsed (see Note)

½ cup roughly chopped Tuscan kale

½ cup peeled, diced carrots

¼ cup diced tomatoes

1 tablespoon tomato paste

1½ cups low-sodium chicken broth or water

1 tablespoon Marash pepper, plus more for garnish

1 teaspoon cumin seed, lightly toasted and crushed

Extra-virgin olive oil for coating

ZHOUG

1 cup cilantro leaves and stems, roughly chopped

1 serrano or jalapeño pepper, roughly chopped

2 cloves garlic

2 teaspoons ground clove

1 teaspoon cumin seed, lightly toasted

Pinch of cardamom powder

½ cup extra-virgin olive oil

Kosher salt

Honey

Flat-leaf parsley leaves for garnish

Note: I use Eden cannellini beans because they're organic and the company doesn't use bisphenol-A (BPA) to line its food cans. A small detail but worth the loyalty.

1. Preheat the oven to 350°F.

2. Place the salmon fillets on a cutting board. Confirm the fillets will fit into each of four oven-safe ceramic bowls. Trim if necessary (you can trim them into circles, if you wish). Season with salt and pepper and drizzle with the olive oil.

3. **For the güveç,** combine the onion, garlic, squash, beans, kale, carrots, tomatoes, tomato paste, broth, Marash pepper, and cumin seeds in a large bowl. Toss until well mixed.

4. Lightly coat the four oven-safe ceramic dishes with olive oil and evenly distribute the vegetable mixture into each bowl. Pour any remaining liquid from the bowl into each of the four dishes.

5. **For the zhoug,** place the cilantro, serrano, garlic, clove, cumin, cardamom, and olive oil into a small food processor or blender. Pulse until smooth. Taste and adjust the seasoning with salt and a little bit of honey. Put three-quarters of the zhoug in a bowl.

6. Set the salmon fillets on top of the vegetables and brush the salmon with the zhoug from the bowl.

7. Place the bowls on a baking sheet and transfer to the oven. Bake for 8 to 10 minutes, until an instant-read thermometer inserted into the salmon is 122°F for wild, 124°F for farmed, or the fish is cooked to desired doneness, 12 to 15 minutes. Remove the baking sheet from the oven. Brush the fillets with the remaining zhoug and garnish with Marash pepper and parsley leaves.

BAKED

SMOKED SALMON PIZZA

WITH CRÈME FRAÎCHE & CREAM CHEESE, CAPERS, GHERKINS & TOMATOES

My pizza results elevated once I purchased a really good home pizza oven—an electric Breville Smart Oven Pizzaiolo. It gets really hot, reading 740°F on my thermocouple. That's super-hot for a home pizza oven. Better still, with proper ventilation, it can be used indoors year-round. I place the oven on a half-sheet pan and then on my stovetop and preheat it under the vent hood, just in case it generates steam and smoke. The pizza in the photo was cooked in this oven. It truly makes a difference. However, you can also use one of the more advanced multiuse "toaster ovens" now available from Breville, Cuisinart, and others. Many of these ovens will reach a solid 450°F temperature and work really well. I serve this as a brunch item and people love it.

SERVES 4

1 pound fresh pizza dough (see Note)

Extra-virgin olive oil

½ cup organic all-purpose flour

2 teaspoons poppy seeds

¼ cup crème fraîche

¼ cup cream cheese, softened

Kosher salt

½ teaspoon freshly ground black pepper, plus more to taste

8 ounces smoked salmon, thinly sliced

8 to 10 cherry tomatoes, halved

4 to 5 gherkins, sliced

2 tablespoons diced red onion

2 teaspoons capers

1 teaspoon sea salt

Flat-leaf parsley leaves and/or dill for garnish (optional)

1. Halve the pizza dough and form each half into a ball. Place each ball into a separate small bowl, rub with olive oil, cover with a towel, and let rest at room temperature for 1 to 2 hours.

2. Preheat the oven to 500°F.

3. Dust a countertop with the flour and roll each ball into a thin oval. Gently pull the oval to ensure it is evenly thick. Let it rest for a few minutes.

4. For a traditional oven, lightly oil two baking sheets and transfer the dough to the sheets. Brush the dough with olive oil and sprinkle each pizza with 1 teaspoon poppy seeds. Bake in the oven at 500°F until golden brown, 8 to 10 minutes. If using a dedicated pizza oven, follow the instructions provided by the manufacturer. Once golden brown, remove from the oven and let rest for 3 to 4 minutes.

5. Meanwhile, in a small bowl, stir together the crème fraîche and cream cheese. Season with kosher salt and pepper. Once the pizzas are baked, spread the mixture across the baked pizza shells.

6. Arrange the smoked salmon on top of the cream cheese spread and garnish both pizzas with the tomatoes, gherkins, onion, and capers. Season each pizza with the sea salt and the ½ teaspoon pepper. Garnish with parsley and/or dill, if desired. Serve at room temperature right from the pan, using a pair of kitchen shears for cutting, or transfer the pizzas to a cutting board and slice into portions before serving.

Note: I make my dough 3 to 4 days prior to cooking and allow it to rest in the refrigerator. The longer you let it rest, the better. You can also purchase fresh pizza dough at a local supermarket and follow the same procedure; rest for 3 to 4 days prior to preparation.

BAKED
SWEDISH-STYLE SALMON MEATBALLS

Swedish meatballs with salmon? Yep! This idea was conceived while visiting IKEA to purchase plates for one of our photo shoots. IKEA sells tons of meatballs and salmon, so the idea seemed logical. These salmon meatballs are succulent and nutritious—a wonderful alternative to the traditional version.

SERVES 4

One 1¼-pound skinless, boneless salmon fillet, cut into several pieces and lightly frozen

3 large egg whites

½ cup heavy whipping cream

1 shallot, minced

1 clove garlic, minced

2 teaspoons kosher salt

1 teaspoon freshly ground black pepper

1 teaspoon ground caraway

1 teaspoon smoked paprika

⅔ cup panko

Mushroom Cream Sauce (recipe follows)

Zest of 1 lemon for garnish

Cooked linguine or steamed rice for serving

1. Preheat the oven to 400°F. Use cooking spray to grease a baking sheet.

2. Place the cold salmon in the bowl of a food processor fitted with the metal blade. Add the egg whites and heavy cream, and pulse for 10 to 15 seconds. Be careful not to over blend; the salmon should retain some texture.

3. Transfer the mixture to a large bowl and use a spatula to fold in the shallot, garlic, salt, pepper, caraway, paprika, and panko. Mix until just combined.

4. Using a large spoon, scoop up 1 to 1½ ounces of the salmon mixture. Wet your hands and roll the salmon mixture between your palms. Place each meatball on the prepared baking sheet. You will make about 20 balls. Once the meatballs are formed, bake until firm and light golden brown on top, 10 to 12 minutes. Remove from the oven and rest for 2 to 3 minutes. Transfer the meatballs to a serving platter.

5. Meanwhile, in a small saucepan, warm the mushroom cream sauce over medium-low heat. Pour the sauce over the meatballs and garnish with lemon zest. Serve with linguine.

MUSHROOM CREAM SAUCE

MAKES ABOUT 3 CUPS

3 tablespoons unsalted butter

2 shallots, minced

⅓ cup dry vermouth

9 ounces white button mushrooms, sliced

2 cups heavy whipping cream

1½ teaspoons ground caraway

1½ teaspoons kosher salt

1 teaspoon ground nutmeg

Pinch of freshly ground black pepper

¼ bunch chives, thinly sliced

¼ bunch dill sprigs, chopped

¼ bunch flat-leaf parsley leaves, chopped

Melt the butter in a medium saucepan over medium-high heat. Add the shallots and sweat until translucent. Deglaze the pan with the vermouth and let simmer until reduced by half. Stir in the mushrooms and cover. Let the mushrooms cook until wilted, about 8 minutes. Add the heavy cream and simmer for 1 to 2 minutes. Add the caraway, salt, nutmeg, and pepper, and simmer over medium heat until the sauce is slightly reduced and thickened, about 10 minutes. Stir in the chives, dill, and parsley.

TAYLOR
HOLD
ON/OFF
-40/450°F
-40/230°C
°F/°C

BROILING

Broiling is a dry-cooking method that uses radiant high heat from above to cook food quickly. It's like grilling, but instead of the heat source being below the food, it comes from above. Most ovens have a broil setting that turns on a heating element in the top of the oven. This creates intense, direct heat that rapidly cooks food and facilitates (yep, I'll say it again) that delicious browning we love. Broiling temperatures are extremely high, usually around 450 to 550°F. This intense heat is what gives food that characteristic browned and slightly charred surface. Broiling is primarily used to brown and crisp the surface of food. It's not ideal for cooking things through, as the high heat can easily burn the outside before the inside is cooked. Keep this in mind. I often broil to brown and then finish the product by flipping the switch to baking mode and a temperature of 325°F. One last point: Broiling requires careful monitoring, as food can go from perfectly browned to burnt very quickly.

HERE ARE SOME BASIC TIPS FOR BROILING:

DRY THE FISH: Pat the salmon dry with paper towels before seasoning and cooking to increase the potential for browning.

SEASON THE FISH: At a minimum, use good-quality salt and pepper. If you have time, lightly cure the fish with salt (or a salt and sugar combination) and refrigerate for 30 minutes.

RUB WITH OIL: Lightly coat the fish with oil. I use good-quality olive oil. Don't use too much oil or it will accelerate browning and increase the risk of burning.

USE THE RIGHT PAN: Use a heavy-duty baking sheet or a small stainless steel sizzle platter lined with oil-rubbed foil.

ADJUST THE RACK: Before preheating, position the oven rack so the food is the appropriate distance from the heating element. Thicker cuts should be farther away, thinner cuts closer. I tend to place the rack in the middle of the oven for even heat and to better control charring.

CONSIDER THE TOPPINGS: Those with high oil content, such as mayonnaise and nuts, will brown quickly, so be extra careful.

WATCH CAREFULLY: Keep a close eye on your food while broiling to prevent burning. Don't be afraid to open the oven and check from time to time.

DON'T OVERCOOK: Salmon cooks quickly, so keep an eye on it. Insert an instant-read digital thermometer in the thickest part of the fillet and take a reading to determine if the fish is cooked (122°F for wild, 124°F for farmed, or to preference). The thickest part of the salmon will be opaque and flake easily with a fork.

PROTECT YOUR HANDS: Use a dry, thick towel or high-heat oven mitts to transfer the pan from the broiler to the stovetop to cool.

LET THE FISH REST: Once the desired temperature is reached, remove the salmon from the oven and let it rest for a few minutes on a plate, skin side up if there is skin.

USE THE RIGHT TOOL: Transfer the fish to a plate using a pair of tongs, a fish spatula, or a metal spatula large enough to lift the fish without it breaking.

OPPOSITE: Salmon fleet at rest, with Mount Verstovia in the background, at Crescent Harbor, in Sitka, Alaska.

EAR
SITKA
NAUTILUS

BROILED SALMON WITH HOT PEPPER JELLY & PEACH SALSA

This easy dish was inspired by the South (because of the peaches) and can come together quickly for final cooking in a toaster oven. I broil using stainless steel skewers, but you can use bamboo skewers instead. The hot pepper jelly is available premade at many supermarkets. I like to serve this dish with steamed jasmine rice and sautéed fennel.

SERVES 4 ✳ COOK TO 122°F FOR WILD, 124°F FOR FARMED, OR TO DESIRED DONENESS

One 12-ounce skinless, boneless salmon fillet, cut into 12 (1-inch) cubes

Extra-virgin olive oil for coating

Kosher salt and freshly ground black pepper

½ cup hot pepper jelly, plus more to taste

Peach Salsa (recipe follows)

1. Soak 4 bamboo skewers in water for 30 minutes. Once soaked, skewer 3 salmon cubes on each skewer. Place the skewers on a foil-lined baking sheet coated with olive oil and season with salt and pepper.

2. Preheat the broiler on high.

3. Place the pepper jelly in a small glass bowl or mug and heat in the microwave for 15 seconds. Spoon or drizzle jelly over the salmon cubes.

4. Broil until lightly golden brown with mild charring in a few spots, about 6 minutes, and an instant-read thermometer inserted into the thickest part of a cube is 122°F for wild, 124°F for farmed, or the fish is cooked to desired doneness.

5. To serve, spoon some peach salsa onto individual plates and top each with the salmon skewers. Drizzle with additional pepper jelly, if desired.

PEACH SALSA

MAKES ABOUT 2 CUPS

3 ripe medium peaches, halved, pitted, and diced into ¼-inch cubes

2 tablespoons minced red onion

2 tablespoons minced fresh mint

¼ cup rice vinegar

¼ cup extra-virgin olive oil

Kosher salt and freshly ground black pepper

In a medium bowl, combine the peaches, onion, mint, vinegar, and olive oil. Stir well to combine and season with salt and pepper. Let sit at room temperature for about 20 minutes before serving. Refrigerate the extra salsa in a small airtight container. It will last 3 to 5 days.

BROILED SALMON WITH LOBSTER SALAD GRATINÉE & WHIPPED CELERY ROOT

While writing this book, I created a whole set of recipes called "duets," where salmon is paired with other types of seafood. Most of the recipes didn't make the cut, but this one with lobster did. The lobster and salmon are delicious together. To make this dish dairy-free, you can substitute the cream with chicken broth blended with 2 teaspoons of margarine. Or you can add extra regular butter or olive oil to the celery root while blending to lighten the texture and make it creamier. I like to add a little lemon zest to the celery root before serving, too. You can use any cut of salmon, but I like the belly because it is higher in fat.

SERVES 4 ✱ COOK TO 122°F FOR WILD, 124°F FOR FARMED, OR TO DESIRED DONENESS

Four 3-ounce skinless, boneless salmon fillets from the belly flap

Kosher salt and freshly ground black pepper

¼ cup extra-virgin olive oil

6 ounces cooked lobster meat (knuckles and claws)

2 ribs celery, finely diced

⅓ cup high-quality mayonnaise

One 1-pound celery root, washed, peeled, and cut into 8 pieces

½ cup heavy cream

Zest of 1 lemon

12 celery leaves for garnish

1. Trim the salmon portions so they are evenly sized and season with salt and pepper. Place the salmon portions on a foil-lined baking sheet and brush with the olive oil. Cover loosely and set aside.

2. Cut the lobster into evenly sized pieces. (Claws usually require cutting; knuckle meat can be left whole.) In a medium bowl, combine the lobster meat with the celery and mayonnaise. Season with salt and pepper. Refrigerate, covered, until ready to use.

3. Place the celery root in a medium saucepan with the heavy cream and bring to a gentle simmer over medium heat. Simmer until the celery root is completely tender, about 20 minutes. Carefully transfer the celery root and poaching liquid to the bowl of a food processor with a metal blade or a blender and process until smooth, creamy, and thick enough to coat the back of a spoon. If using a blender, hold the lid closed with a towel while processing as hot liquid will expand. Season with salt, pepper, and lemon zest.

4. Preheat the broiler on high.

5. Uncover the baking sheet and broil the salmon until rare in the center, around 115°F, 3 to 5 minutes. Remove the baking sheet from the oven and spoon 1 or 2 tablespoons of the lobster salad on top of each salmon portion. Return the pan to the broiler and broil until the lobster salad is golden brown, 3 to 4 minutes, and an instant-read thermometer inserted in the thickest part of the salmon is 122°F for wild, 124°F for farmed, or the fish is cooked to desired doneness. Watch carefully as the lobster browns quickly.

6. To serve, spoon celery root puree onto each of four serving plates. Using a fish spatula, carefully place each portion of salmon on the celery root puree. Garnish with celery leaves.

BROILED SALMON WITH FILIPINO PANCIT NOODLES

Although pork and chicken are the traditional proteins used in this Filipino dish, salmon offers a wonderful and healthy twist. The result is savory, unique, and delicious due in part to the Chinese Lap Cheong sausage. Lap Cheong is dry-cured and Cantonese in origin. I prefer the nitrate-free version and use it in limited quantity—just enough to add flavor without overpowering the dish. A little bit goes a long way. Like many noodle dishes, you can store the finished pancit in the refrigerator overnight and it will be better the following day. Reheat in the microwave and it's ready.

SERVES 4 ✳ COOK TO 122°F FOR WILD, 124°F FOR FARMED, OR TO DESIRED DONENESS

PANCIT NOODLES

¼ cup soybean oil

3 large carrots, peeled and julienned on a mandoline

2 ribs celery, julienned on a mandoline

1 medium white onion, julienned

1 small head napa cabbage, shredded

3 ounces Chinese Lap Cheong sausage, julienned

2 cloves garlic, minced

1 pound rice noodles, soaked in cold water for 20 minutes, then drained

½ cup low-sodium soy sauce

¼ cup oyster sauce

½ cup low-sodium chicken broth or water

Kosher salt and freshly ground black pepper

SALMON

One 1-pound skin-on, boneless salmon belly fillet, cut into 4 portions

2 tablespoons maple sugar or light brown sugar

2 tablespoons low-sodium soy sauce

1 teaspoon powdered ginger

Extra-virgin olive oil for coating

---

4 scallions sliced into thin rounds; 4 lime wedges; and 4 branches of steamed broccoli rabe

1. **For the pancit,** pour the oil into a large sauté pan set over medium heat. Once the oil is hot, add the carrots, celery, and onion and sauté until tender, 3 to 4 minutes. Add the cabbage and continue to sauté until the vegetables are tender and lightly golden brown. Transfer the sautéed vegetables to a large bowl and set aside.

2. In the same sauté pan, add the sausage and sauté over medium heat until golden brown, 3 to 4 minutes. Add the garlic and sauté until golden brown, 2 to 3 minutes. Add the soaked noodles to the pan and toss to combine. Add the soy sauce, oyster sauce, and broth and toss to combine. Reduce the heat and cook gently until the noodles are tender, about 8 minutes.

3. Transfer the vegetables back to the sauté pan and toss with the noodles. Cook until the entire mixture is warmed through. Season with salt and pepper.

4. **For the salmon,** preheat the broiler on high. Place the salmon in a large, chilled bowl. In a small bowl, combine the maple sugar, soy sauce, and ginger. Coat the fish all over with this mixture. Transfer the salmon, skin side down, to a foil-lined baking sheet coated with olive oil. Broil until golden brown, 4 to 5 minutes, and an instant-read thermometer inserted in the thickest part of a fillet is 122°F for wild, 124°F for farmed, or the fish is cooked to desired doneness.

5. To serve, divide the pancit among four plates. Top each bowl with a portion of salmon and garnish with the scallions, a lime wedge, and broccoli rabe.

BROILED SALMON RAMEN

Salmon ramen is so delicious and easy to make but often takes a back seat to the traditional chicken or pork options. This recipe uses a hybrid ramen base made of vegetable broth infused with traditional dashi. In Japan, premade dashi base comes conveniently packed in what look like large tea bags—ready to steep in hot liquid. I found my favorite source while wandering around Toyosu Market in Tokyo during a cool autumn morning—the venerable Dashi Okume. Their classic salt-free dashi works perfectly for this recipe and can be purchased online or at their US store in Brooklyn, New York.

SERVES 4 ✳ COOK TO 122°F FOR WILD, 124°F FOR FARMED, OR TO DESIRED DONENESS

Four 4-ounce skin-on, boneless center-cut salmon fillets

1 teaspoon kosher salt

2 tablespoons avocado oil

5 ounces shiitake mushrooms, stems removed, thinly sliced

4 scallions, cut into ½-inch segments

One 1-inch knob ginger, julienned

2 tablespoons white miso

6 cups low-sodium vegetable broth

4 bags Dashi Okume Classic Salt-Free Dashi

Two 3-ounce packages ramen noodles

2 ounces baby kale or spinach (about 2 cups)

1 cup shredded carrot

Extra-virgin olive oil for coating

1 tablespoon Japanese dipping sauce, such as Bachan's (see Note)

1. Season the salmon with the salt and allow to rest for 8 to 10 minutes.

2. Heat the avocado oil in a large pot over medium-high heat until shimmering.

3. Add the mushrooms, scallions, and ginger and stir. Cover, reduce the heat to medium, and allow to cook for 3 to 4 minutes, stirring occasionally. Remove the lid and add the white miso, stirring and allowing it to brown lightly as the pan dries out.

4. Add the vegetable broth and bring to a simmer. Add the dashi broth bags and simmer for 6 to 7 minutes. Using a slotted spoon, carefully remove the dashi broth bags without breaking them. Discard the bags.

5. Add the noodles, kale, and carrot to the broth and stir. Simmer on low until the noodles are tender (follow the cooking time noted on the ramen packaging), about 4 minutes. Fully cooked noodles should still have some spring and texture to them.

6. Preheat the broiler on high. Place the salmon fillets, skin side up, on a foil-lined baking sheet coated with olive oil. Drizzle with the dipping sauce; be sure they are coated evenly to prevent burning. Broil until the skin is golden brown, 7 to 8 minutes, and an instant-read thermometer inserted in the thickest part of a fillet is 122°F for wild, 124°F for farmed, or the fish is cooked to desired doneness. The fish can be broiled with or without skewers.

7. To serve, ladle ½ cup broth into each serving bowl. Using tongs, portion out ½ cup ramen noodles along with some of the mushrooms, kale, and carrot. Place a salmon fillet on top.

Notes:

You can make your own Japanese dipping sauce by combining the following in a medium saucepan over medium heat: 1 cup tamari, ¼ cup mirin, ¼ cup rice vinegar, ¼ cup granulated sugar, 1 tablespoon grated garlic, 1 tablespoon grated fresh ginger, 1 tablespoon sesame paste, and 1 teaspoon white miso. Bring to a simmer and reduce to desired thickness. Transfer to a mason jar and allow to cool, uncovered, to room temperature. Refrigerate, covered, for up to 1 week.

If desired, you can add a common Japanese ramen topping—a slice of narutomaki, a fish cake.

BROILED SALMON WITH TABBOULEH GRATINÉE & ZHOUG EMULSION

This is another recipe inspired by Eastern Mediterranean and Middle Eastern flavors, though salmon is not a traditional ingredient. Tabbouleh includes ingredients like tomatoes, herbs, olive oil, and lemon, which complements the salmon. Zhoug originated in Yemen and uses a pepper base. The tabbouleh and zhoug pair wonderfully with the salmon. I like to serve the salmon with sliced roasted golden beets, a spicy cucumber salad, and a garnish of fresh herbs.

SERVES 4 ✳ COOK TO 122°F FOR WILD, 124°F FOR FARMED, OR TO DESIRED DONENESS

TABBOULEH GRATINÉE

¼ cup fine bulgur wheat

1 clove garlic, blanched (see Notes) and minced

½ cup roughly chopped flat-leaf parsley stems and leaves

½ cup roughly chopped fresh mint stems and leaves

¼ cup finely chopped fresh plum tomatoes

1 shallot, peeled and minced

Zest and juice of 1 lemon

½ teaspoon kosher salt

½ teaspoon freshly ground black pepper

½ cup mayonnaise

ZHOUG EMULSION

3 poblano peppers, charred, peeled, and seeded (see Notes)

2 medium jalapeño peppers, charred, peeled, and seeded (see Notes)

1 cup roughly chopped cilantro stems and leaves

1 cup roughly chopped flat-leaf parsley stems and leaves

2 cloves garlic, blanched (see Notes)

1 teaspoon kosher salt, plus more to taste

1 teaspoon ground coriander

1 teaspoon ground cumin

⅓ cup extra-virgin olive oil

¼ cup rice vinegar

Freshly ground black pepper

SALMON

Four 4-ounce skinless, boneless salmon fillets

2 tablespoons extra-virgin olive oil

1. **For the tabbouleh,** place the bulgur wheat in a glass bowl and cover with warm water. Soak for 30 minutes, then drain through a fine-mesh sieve. Return to the bowl and add the garlic, parsley, mint, tomatoes, shallot, and lemon zest. Season with the salt, pepper, and some of the lemon juice, then taste and adjust as needed. Stir in the mayonnaise, combining until smooth and spreadable. Transfer to a small airtight container and refrigerate for 30 minutes to allow the flavors to meld.

2. **For the zhoug,** blot the peppers with paper towels, then place in a blender with the herbs, garlic, salt, coriander, and cumin. Blend on medium speed. While the blender is running, drizzle in the olive oil, then the vinegar. Increase to high speed and blend until smooth. Stop the blender, add pepper, then taste and adjust seasonings and texture by adding more salt and pepper or additional oil and vinegar. Store the zhoug emulsion in an airtight container in the refrigerator for 30 minutes or up to 5 days.

3. Preheat the broiler on low.

4. **For the salmon,** place the fillets on a foil-lined baking sheet and rub all over with the olive oil. Spread ⅓ cup of the tabbouleh mixture on top of each portion of salmon. Broil until the tabbouleh is golden brown, 8 to 10 minutes, and an instant-read thermometer inserted in the thickest part of a fillet is 122°F for wild, 124°F for farmed, or the fish is cooked to desired doneness.

5. To serve, spoon ¼ cup of the zhoug into each of four bowls. Top with a fillet of salmon and tabbouleh gratinée and serve at once.

Notes:

To blanch garlic, microwave on high for 15 to 20 seconds to soften and cut the sharp flavor.

To char and peel peppers, use the flame on a gas stovetop, a grill, or a broiler heated on high to completely char the peppers. Once charred, transfer to a glass bowl and cover tightly with plastic wrap. Allow the peppers to cool, about 10 minutes. Remove the plastic wrap and use a paper towel or cold running water to remove the skins. Use a knife to scrape away the seeds and stems.

BROILED SALMON WITH CRANBERRY-ALMOND CHERMOULA

Chermoula is a classic North African preparation that includes herbs like parsley, cilantro, and mint, along with citrus and garlic. It is used to season fish and poultry and is quite similar to an Argentinian chimichurri. This recipe is a riff that adds dried cranberries for tartness and toasted almond slivers. Serve with stewed chickpeas or your favorite rice or vegetable side.

SERVES 2 ✳ COOK TO 122°F FOR WILD, 124°F FOR FARMED, OR TO DESIRED DONENESS

Two 4-ounce skin-on, boneless salmon fillets

Kosher salt and freshly ground black pepper

¾ cup extra-virgin olive oil, plus more for coating and drizzling

1 cup almond slivers, toasted

½ cup dried cranberries

½ cup minced shallot, microwaved for 20 seconds on high to soften

1 small bunch cilantro leaves and stems

1 small bunch mint

3 cloves garlic, minced, microwaved for 20 seconds on high to soften

Juice of 2 limes, plus more as needed

1½ teaspoons saffron, soaked in 1 tablespoon warm water

1. Set the salmon fillets on a plate and season with salt and pepper. Drizzle 2 to 3 tablespoons olive oil over the top. Cover loosely with plastic wrap and refrigerate for 30 minutes.

2. Put ½ cup of the almond slivers in a medium bowl along with the cranberries and shallot and set aside.

3. Place the remaining almonds in the bowl of a food processor. Add the cilantro, mint, garlic, lime juice, ¾ cup olive oil, and saffron with water and pulse until the mixture is smooth. Fold the pureed herb mixture into the bowl with the reserved almond mixture. Stir until incorporated. Taste and adjust the seasoning with salt, pepper, and more lime juice as needed.

4. Preheat the broiler on low.

5. Transfer the salmon, skin side down, to a foil-lined baking sheet coated with olive oil. Top each fillet with 1 to 2 tablespoons of the chermoula. Broil until the chermoula is lightly browned, 8 to 10 minutes, and an instant-read thermometer inserted in the thickest part of a fillet is 122°F for wild, 124°F for farmed, or the fish is cooked to desired doneness. Rest on a plate for 2 to 3 minutes before serving.

BROILED SALMON ON INJERA BREAD WITH LENTIL DRESSING

Years ago, I was hired to help produce a series of recipes and images for a national culinary magazine, and one of them was for a dish that used injera bread. I had never fermented a batch of injera batter but found the process easy and the result tangy and delicious. Like many ferments, injera batter is best when produced in two stages beginning with a starter, or *ersho*. Once the ersho is tangy and developed, it is used to start a full batch. When finished, I save a half cup of batter as the ersho for the next batch of injera—kind of like sourdough.

SERVES 4 ✳ COOK TO 122°F FOR WILD, 124°F FOR FARMED, OR TO DESIRED DONENESS

ERSHO STARTER

- ½ cup teff flour
- 1 cup water

BATTER

- 1½ cups ersho starter
- 2½ cups teff flour
- 2 cups lukewarm water
- 1 tablespoon extra-virgin olive oil

LENTIL DRESSING

- ½ cup cooked yellow lentils
- ¼ cup mayonnaise
- 2 tablespoons freshly squeezed lemon juice
- 1 tablespoon olive oil
- 1 clove garlic, minced
- 1 teaspoon ground cumin
- Kosher salt and freshly ground black pepper

SALMON

- One 1-pound skinless, boneless salmon belly flap, cut into 4 portions
- 1 teaspoon kosher salt
- Extra-virgin olive oil
- ½ teaspoon ground coriander
- ½ teaspoon ground ginger

- ¼ cup thinly sliced scallions
- ¼ cup Anaheim peppers (see Notes, page 87), chopped
- 1 tablespoon roughly chopped flat-leaf parsley leaves

1. **For the ersho starter,** combine the teff flour and water in a plastic container, mixing until smooth. Cover loosely with a kitchen towel and let it ferment at room temperature for 2 to 3 days, or until it develops a slightly sour aroma and bubbly surface.

2. **For the batter,** once the ersho starter is ready, transfer the 1½ cups to a blender. Add the teff flour and water and blend until you achieve a smooth, thin batter, similar to pancake batter.

3. Pour the blended batter into a clean container, cover loosely with a kitchen towel, and let it ferment at room temperature for another 1 to 2 days. The fermentation time can vary based on temperature and desired sourness. You'll see small bubbles forming on the surface as it ferments. This is the final fermentation. When fermentation is complete, the batter will have a slightly sour aroma and a frothy consistency.

4. Heat a large, flat griddle or crêpe pan. Brush with 1 tablespoon olive oil. Pour a ladleful of the batter onto the hot surface, swirling to create a thin, even circle about 7 inches in diameter. Cook until small holes appear on the surface and the edges lift, and the injera is set and cooked through, about 5 minutes. Continue the process until you have four pancakes. Refrigerate the remaining batter in an airtight plastic container as a starter for your next batch.

5. **For the lentil dressing,** place the lentils, mayonnaise, lemon juice, olive oil, garlic, and cumin in a blender and process until smooth and creamy. If necessary, add water, 1 tablespoon at a time while blending, until it reaches your desired consistency. The texture should be similar to a creamy salad dressing. Season with salt and black pepper. Place in a small airtight container and refrigerate until ready to assemble.

6. **For the salmon,** rub the salmon fillets with the salt and refrigerate on a plate, covered, for up to 1 hour until ready to cook.

7. Preheat the broiler on high.

8. Coat a foil-lined baking sheet with olive oil and set the salmon on it, drizzling the fillets with a little more oil. Dust with the coriander and ginger. Broil until deeply golden, 5 to 6 minutes, and an instant-read thermometer inserted in the thickest part of a fillet is 122°F for wild, 124°F for farmed, or the fish is cooked to desired doneness.

9. To serve, lay a pancake flat on a plate. Top with 2 tablespoons of the lentil dressing and spread it around the center of the pancake. Place a piece of broiled salmon in the center of the pancake. Sprinkle with scallion, Anaheim pepper, and parsley and fold into a half-moon. Repeat with the remaining servings.

BROILED SALMON WITH TUSCAN TOMATO & BREAD PANZANELLA SALAD

This is truly a salad for summer, when tomatoes are at their peak and the salmon is available at its freshest. Salmon pairs well with the herbaceous vinaigrette base to this salad. Feel free to mix and match the fresh herb components by replacing the basil with cilantro, tarragon, fennel fronds, or scallions (or a mixture). There will be plenty of leftover salad to enjoy afterward.

SERVES 4 ✳ COOK TO 122°F FOR WILD, 124°F FOR FARMED, OR TO DESIRED DONENESS

½ loaf ciabatta bread, cut into ½-inch cubes (roughly 3 cups)

One 15½-ounce can cannellini beans, drained and rinsed

3 ripe globe tomatoes, cut into thin wedges

1 pint cherry tomatoes, halved

1 cup fresh basil leaves

1 cup flat-leaf parsley leaves

1 clove garlic

2 tablespoons balsamic vinegar

½ cup extra-virgin olive oil, plus more for coating and drizzling

Four 3-ounce skinless, boneless salmon fillets

Kosher salt and freshly ground black pepper

1. In a large bowl, combine the bread, beans, and tomatoes, stirring gently to combine.

2. In the bowl of a food processor fitted with the metal blade, combine the basil, parsley, garlic, balsamic vinegar, and ⅓ cup of the olive oil and pulse for 10 seconds until emulsified.

3. Pour the marinade over the bread mixture and toss to combine. Allow to marinate at room temperature for 30 minutes.

4. Preheat the broiler on high.

5. Place the salmon fillets on a foil-lined baking sheet coated with olive oil. Season with salt and pepper and drizzle with the remaining olive oil. Broil until golden brown, about 6 minutes, and an instant-read thermometer inserted in the thickest part of a fillet is 122°F for wild, 124°F for farmed, or the fish is cooked to desired doneness.

6. Spoon the tomato bread salad into four serving bowls and top each bowl with a salmon fillet.

BROILED SALMON CHACARERO SANDWICH

A *chacarero* is a traditional Chilean sandwich usually made with thinly sliced beef served on a round roll with tomatoes, thinly sliced green beans, sliced ripe tomato, a healthy dollop of mayonnaise, and a dusting of Merkén chili pepper. It is one of the many varieties of sandwich served in Chilean *fuentes de soda*, or *schoperías*—restaurants equivalent to an American diner or "greasy spoon." Here, I replace the traditional meat with Chilean steelhead salmon for a healthy alternative.

SERVES 4 ✳ COOK TO 122°F FOR WILD, 124°F FOR FARMED, OR TO DESIRED DONENESS

Four 2-ounce skinless, boneless salmon fillets

2 teaspoons Merkén pepper or chipotle chili powder

Kosher salt and freshly ground black pepper

2 tablespoons extra-virgin olive oil

4 slider buns

4 tomato slices (about the same diameter as the buns)

¼ cup mayonnaise

½ cup guacamole

½ cup green beans, blanched and julienned

1. Preheat the broiler on high.

2. Dust the salmon with the Merkén, salt, and pepper. Coat all over with the olive oil. Place on a foil-lined baking sheet. Broil until golden brown and an instant-read thermometer inserted in the thickest part of a fillet is 122°F for wild, 124°F for farmed, or the fish is cooked to desired doneness, 5 to 6 minutes. Allow to rest for 3 to 4 minutes, then slice.

3. To assemble, lay the bottom buns on a platter. Place a tomato slice on each bottom bun and top each with slices of salmon. Add a liberal scoop of mayonnaise and guacamole and top with blanched green beans. The slightly underbaked bun, liberal scoop of mayonnaise, and topping of green beans are typical to the original served in Chile.

BROILED

SALMON, EGG & CHICKPEA SHAKSHUKA

Shakshuka is a North African and Middle Eastern one-pot pepper, tomato, and egg dish. I modify it by adding chickpeas and salmon, and I serve it as a brunch option. Most of the ingredients are easy to find. You can buy harissa powder online or substitute hot paprika or cayenne pepper.

SERVES 4 ✳ COOK TO 122°F FOR WILD, 124°F FOR FARMED, OR TO DESIRED DONENESS

- One 12-ounce skinless, boneless salmon fillet, cut into 2- or 3-inch portions
- 1 tablespoon kosher salt, plus more to taste
- 2 teaspoons harissa powder
- ¼ cup extra-virgin olive oil, plus more for coating
- 1 red bell pepper, charred and peeled (see Notes, page 87)
- 1 yellow bell pepper, charred and peeled (see Notes, page 87)
- 1 poblano pepper, charred and peeled (see Notes, page 87)
- 1 small yellow onion, diced
- 2 cloves garlic, minced
- 1 teaspoon ground cumin
- 1 teaspoon sweet paprika
- ½ teaspoon ground turmeric
- ¼ teaspoon ground cardamom
- One 28-ounce can whole plum tomatoes with their juices
- One 15½-ounce can chickpeas
- Freshly ground black pepper
- 4 large eggs
- Toasted pita bread for serving

1. Season the salmon with 1 tablespoon salt and the harissa powder and set aside on a foil-lined baking sheet coated with olive oil. Chop the peppers.

2. In a medium saucepan, heat the ¼ cup olive oil over medium heat. Add the onion and garlic and sauté until softened, 4 to 5 minutes. Add the chopped peppers, cumin, paprika, turmeric, and cardamom and continue cooking until heated through. Add the tomatoes and bring to a simmer. Remove the pan from the heat.

3. Using an immersion blender, blend the tomato mixture until partially chopped but not smooth. (Alternatively, carefully transfer the mixture to a blender and blend until smooth. Be careful, as hot liquids will expand. Once blended, return the mixture to the saucepan.)

4. Stir in the chickpeas and season with salt and pepper. Place the saucepan back over medium heat. Crack the eggs into individual spots atop the shakshuka mixture, season with salt and pepper, and cook until the eggs are set or to your desired doneness.

5. Meanwhile, preheat a broiler on high. Broil the salmon until golden brown, 4 to 6 minutes, and an instant-read thermometer inserted in the thickest part of a fillet is 122°F for wild, 124°F for farmed, or the fish is cooked to desired doneness.

6. To serve, spoon one egg and the shakshuka mixture onto each of four plates (the photo shows two portions on a serving plate). Top each with a piece of salmon and serve with toasted pita bread.

CURING

Curing salmon involves salting and brining the fish to improve its flavor, texture, and shelf life. As mentioned earlier (see page 41), it helps reduce the amount of albumin that naturally leaks from the salmon and reduces splatter in the pan during cooking. Brief curing, a technique where the fish is lightly salted, is recommended before cooking salmon in general. Most of the recipes in this book suggest briefly curing the salmon before cooking. Long curing is a technique where the fish does not undergo additional cooking—the cure is the final step before consumption.

When curing salmon, much depends on the amount and ratio of salt and sugar used. The lower the ratio of salt, the sweeter. A lower ratio of curing mixture to fish set for a shorter period of time yields a lighter and creamier result but a shorter shelf life. A higher ratio of cure to fish set over a longer period of time results in a firmer finished product with a longer shelf life. The process lowers the level of water in the fillet, causing it to firm up. The decreased water level is what preserves the fish.

THERE ARE TWO WAYS TO CURE FISH: A WET BRINE OR A DRY BRINE.

WET BRINE: The salmon is submerged in a liquid solution of salt, sugar, and water. My preferred ratio of salt and sugar in a wet brine is 1.5 percent salt and 1.5 percent sugar by weight of the salmon, which is approximately ½ ounce sugar and ½ ounce salt, or about 3 teaspoons of each. Note that the measure doesn't have to be perfect.

DRY BRINING: The salmon is covered with a dry mixture of salt, sugar, and sometimes other seasonings. For a 2-pound side of salmon, I use 2 tablespoons kosher salt and 2 tablespoons organic granulated sugar spread evenly over the fillet, and I cure for at least 24 hours in the refrigerator.

These recipes use a dry-brine process for simplicity, performance, and sanitation. I am not a huge fan of placing fish fillets in water.

GENERAL GUIDELINES FOR DRY CURING INCLUDE:

- Be sure to sufficiently cover the fish fillet with the curing mixture.
- Follow guidelines for the length of time the fish cures—the longer the cure, the firmer the fish (and the longer the shelf life when done).
- Always rinse the curing mixture off of the fish in ice-cold running water when curing is finished.
- Pat the fish dry with paper towels and wrap tightly in plastic wrap after rinsing, if not serving immediately.
- Store in the refrigerator until you are ready to use it.
- This is a raw food that will not undergo additional cooking before consumption, so always handle with strict attention to sanitation and food safety.

OPPOSITE: A steelhead salmon-farming site at the eastern end of Reloncaví Estuary in Los Lagos, Chile.

CURED SALMON ON AVOCADO TOAST

Avocado toast has become synonymous with breakfast and snacks. This light, refreshing breakfast starter incorporates the sweet flavors of cured salmon, a slight acidic note from the citrus, and herbal and floral combinations from the seasonal garnish. I provide an easy method for curing salmon here, but you could also use store-bought smoked salmon.

SERVES 4 ✱ CURE TIME: 24 HOURS

CURED SALMON

1 tablespoon kosher salt

1 tablespoon granulated sugar

Freshly ground black pepper

Zest and juice of 1 lemon

One 8-ounce skinless, boneless loin-cut salmon fillet

AVOCADO SMASH

2 avocados, halved and pitted

2 tablespoons freshly squeezed lime juice

1½ teaspoons kosher salt

ASSEMBLY

1 tablespoon extra-virgin olive oil, plus more for drizzling

4 slices sourdough bread

¼ cup thinly sliced radish

6 Japanese cucumbers, thinly sliced

12 thin slices cured salmon

Edible flowers for garnish

Maldon flaky sea salt

1. **For the cured salmon,** combine the salt, sugar, a pinch of pepper, and lemon zest and juice in a small bowl. Cover a baking sheet with a piece of plastic wrap and pour half of the mixture on the plastic. Place the salmon on top of the curing mixture and cover with the remaining cure; cover tightly in the plastic wrap. Place the wrapped salmon in a plastic container large enough to fit the fillet and press with a weight (such as a plate). Refrigerate for 24 hours.

2. Once cured, unwrap the salmon and rinse under ice-cold running water to remove the cure; pat dry with paper towels. Use a sharp knife to thinly slice the salmon at an angle. You will need 12 slices.

3. **For the avocado smash,** scoop out the avocado into a medium bowl and add the lime juice and salt. Using a fork, gently smash the ingredients together, keeping some large chunks of avocado.

4. **For the assembly,** in a medium skillet heat the olive oil over medium heat. Add 2 of the sourdough slices and toast until a golden-brown crust forms, then flip to toast the other sides. Repeat with the remaining slices.

5. Place an equal amount of the avocado smash on top of each slice. Decorate with sliced radish, cucumber, and 3 cured salmon slices, then top with edible flowers. Sprinkle with sea salt and drizzle with olive oil.

CURED SALMON WITH EGG & AVOCADO ON A BAGEL

This is a lighter curing blend and results in a moist, creamy texture, not as firm as a cure that uses a higher quantity of salt and sugar. You can experiment with salt and sugar ratios, curing times, and flavorings, too. I often add a pinch of powdered ginger to enhance the cure. Don't be shy when it comes to trying new things.

SERVES 4 ✳ CURE TIME: 24 HOURS

2 tablespoons granulated sugar

1 tablespoon kosher salt, plus more to taste

½ teaspoon ginger powder

One 12-ounce skin-on, boneless loin-cut salmon fillet

2 ripe avocados, halved and pitted

Juice of 1 lime

1 tablespoon minced flat-leaf parsley leaves

Freshly ground black pepper

8 large eggs

¼ cup extra-virgin olive oil

4 everything or plain bagels, halved and toasted

4 sprigs dill for garnish

1 teaspoon thinly sliced fresh chives for garnish

1. In a small bowl, combine the sugar, 1 tablespoon salt, and ginger. Place the salmon in a glass baking dish and season liberally with the cure. Cover the dish with plastic wrap and refrigerate for 24 hours.

2. Once cured, unwrap the salmon and rinse under ice-cold running water to remove the cure; pat dry with paper towels. Using a very sharp knife, thinly slice the salmon against the grain on an angle; you will need 16 to 24 slices. Place the slices on a plate as you go. Slice the entire fillet. (Cover any leftover salmon slices in plastic wrap and store in the refrigerator for 3 to 4 days.)

3. Gently scoop the avocado flesh into a medium bowl. Add the lime juice and parsley. Mash with a fork until mostly smooth with some chunks. Season the smashed avocado with salt and pepper and set aside.

4. Crack the eggs into a large bowl and beat until smooth. Heat the olive oil in a nonstick pan over medium-high heat. Add the eggs and cook, stirring gently, until firm. Season with salt and pepper.

5. Assemble the dish by dividing the avocado mixture on the toasted bagel halves, followed by the egg. Finish by topping each with 2 or 3 slices of salmon. Garnish with fresh dill and chives, and serve.

CURED

SALMON LOX, CAVIAR & HERBS

I love serving fresh salmon lox with sturgeon caviar: The flavor is a match made in heaven. However, I also recognize the expense, so feel free to substitute ikura salmon roe or forgo the caviar altogether. If you do include the caviar, it is available at high-end retailers and online. A little bit of caviar goes a long way, so use it judiciously. One of my favorite sustainable sturgeon caviars, which is relatively affordable, is the Siberian Classic by Calvisius. You can order it at calvisiususa.com.

SERVES 4 ✱ CURE TIME: 24 TO 48 HOURS

One 1-pound skin-on, boneless salmon fillet, preferably from head end

¼ cup kosher salt

¼ cup granulated sugar

¼ cup chopped fresh dill

2½ tablespoons sturgeon caviar

¼ cup baby herb sprouts (see Note) for garnish

¼ cup shaved red onion for garnish

1. Prepare the lox by lining a small shallow bowl or rimmed pan with plastic wrap. Place the salmon skin side down on the plastic wrap and spread the salt, sugar, and dill evenly over the salmon. Press the cure gently into the salmon so it adheres. Cover with a second sheet of plastic wrap and place the salmon in the refrigerator to cure for 24 to 48 hours, depending on the thickness of the salmon. For a typical 1½-inch-thick fillet of salmon, I cure for at least 24 hours.

2. Once cured, unwrap the salmon and rinse under ice-cold running water to remove the cure; pat dry with paper towels. Using a sharp knife, slice the salmon against the grain as thinly as possible from the head toward the tail end. Angle the knife so the blade slides along the inside surface of the skin once through the thick part of the fillet. Do not cut through the skin. Detach the slice from the skin using the knife and stack the slices as you continue to cut. Once the fillet is sliced, discard the skin.

3. Roll each slice of salmon into a small coronet or triangle and place on a serving platter. Randomly top the salmon with ¼-teaspoon dollops of caviar. Garnish with baby herb sprouts and onion.

Note: I used baby herbs from Chef's Garden in Huron, Ohio, but you can use sprouting greens available at your local supermarket.

CURED SALMON, SAUERKRAUT & JULIENNED SUMMER VEGETABLES

As a food-service professional, I am fortunate enough to interact with some of the best chefs in the world. This often leads to inspiration, and such is the case for this recipe. It was inspired by Chef Junghyun Park of Atomix in New York City. He is amazing with tremendous talent. So, I give credit where credit is due. Though I make my own sauerkraut in autumn, you can use a quality store-bought version. For the baby cucumbers with blossoms, the Chef's Garden in Huron, Ohio, is a reliable online source. Honey powder can be found online, too—just make sure it's pure and isn't made with dried corn syrup.

SERVES 4 * CURE TIME: 24 HOURS

CURED SALMON

1 tablespoon kosher salt

2 tablespoons granulated sugar

1 tablespoon celery salt

One 12-ounce skinless, boneless loin-cut salmon fillet

VEGETABLES

One 16-ounce jar raw sauerkraut

1 large white carrot, peeled and julienned on a mandoline

1 medium cucumber, cut into thin rounds on a mandoline

1 medium summer squash, julienned on a mandoline

1 teaspoon honey powder

Kosher salt and freshly ground pepper

1 package baby cucumbers with blossoms

1. **For the cured salmon,** combine the salt, sugar, and celery salt in a small bowl. Place a piece of plastic wrap on a baking sheet and pour half of the salt mixture onto the plastic. Place the salmon on top of the cure and cover with the remaining mixture. Seal tightly in plastic wrap. Place the wrapped salmon in a plastic container large enough to fit the fillet and press with a weight (such as a plate). Refrigerate for 24 hours.

2. Once cured, unwrap the salmon and rinse under ice-cold running water to remove the cure. Pat dry with paper towels, wrap in plastic, and refrigerate until ready to serve.

3. **For the vegetables,** put the sauerkraut into a bowl. Add the carrot, cucumber, squash, and honey powder and toss to combine. Season with salt and pepper. Refrigerate for at least 2 to 3 hours, or up to 12 hours. Prior to serving, taste the cabbage mixture and adjust the seasoning, if necessary, by adding more salt, pepper, and/or honey powder. You do not want the flavor to be too acidic.

4. To serve, thinly slice the salmon against the grain on an extreme angle (I prefer wide, thin slices for this dish). You will need 8 to 12 slices. Scoop ¼ cup of the vegetable mixture into each of four bowls and drizzle each with 1 tablespoon of the liquid. Top with two or three slices of salmon, garnish with the baby cucumbers, and serve.

BEET-CURED SALMON GRAVLAX TARTINE

As noted earlier, curing is a process where salmon is coated with salt (and sometimes sugar) to draw out moisture via osmosis. The process reduces the amount of water in the fillet, causing it become firm. It also helps preserve the fish. When you rub the fish with a colorful herb or vegetable during the curing process, the color infuses during the process of osmosis. If you have a vacuum sealer, use it to package the salmon instead of a zip-top bag; the vacuum pressure will help accelerate the curing process.

SERVES 4 ✳ CURE TIME: 48 HOURS

CURED SALMON

2 tablespoons kosher salt

3 tablespoons granulated sugar

One 1-pound skinless, boneless loin-cut salmon fillet

2 tablespoons freshly grated red beet

ASSEMBLY

¼ cup thinly sliced red onion

¼ cup rice vinegar

4 teaspoons herbed cream cheese

2 brioche buns, halved and toasted

1 tablespoon dill leaves

1 tablespoon finely sliced chives

1 tablespoon capers

Citrus crystal leaves

1. **For the cured salmon,** combine the salt and sugar in a small bowl. Place the salmon on a plate and coat both sides generously with the grated beets. Season with the salt-sugar mixture. Transfer the salmon to a zip-top bag or vacuum seal in a plastic bag. Refrigerate for 48 hours.

2. Once cured, remove the salmon from the bag and rinse under ice-cold running water to remove the cure. Pat dry with paper towels, wrap in plastic, and refrigerate until ready to serve. (Once rinsed and dried, the salmon can be stored in an airtight container in the refrigerator for 3 to 5 days.)

3. If using immediately, place the salmon in the freezer for 30 to 45 minutes to firm it up (it should be firm but not frozen). Freezing helps with the slicing process. Using a sharp knife, slice the salmon fillet at an angle into 8 to 12 very thin slices.

4. **For the assembly,** combine the onion and vinegar in a small bowl and pickle for 10 minutes.

5. Spread 1 teaspoon of the cream cheese on each bun. Top with 2 or 3 slices of the cured salmon. Garnish with the pickled onions, dill, chives, capers, and citrus crystal leaves, and serve.

BEET-CURED SALMON WITH POTATO & EGG TERRINE

Beet-cured salmon is so stunning and delicious. It is also super easy to make and a real crowd pleaser. Thus, I'm including a second option for serving it—this time with a creamy potato and egg terrine. This is an upscale recipe that requires time, but the cured salmon can be made ahead and cut to order. For alternative cures, you can substitute the beets with other flavorful options like fresh herbs, finely grated carrots, or fresh grated ginger and lemongrass.

SERVES 4

Kosher salt

1 medium Yukon Gold potato, diced (roughly 1 cup)

¼ cup heavy cream

½ gelatin sheet, rehydrated

2 tablespoons crème fraîche

1 hard-boiled egg, diced

1 teaspoon thinly sliced chives

1 teaspoon chopped dill sprigs

1 teaspoon capers

1 bunch frisée, picked into small sprigs

1 tablespoon extra-virgin olive oil

Maldon flaky sea salt

Freshly ground black pepper

16 thin slices of Beet-Cured Salmon (see recipe, page 110)

1. In a small saucepan of salted boiling water, blanch the potato until tender, about 4 minutes. Prepare an ice-water bath. Strain the potatoes and place in the ice-water bath until the potatoes cool. Strain and set aside.

2. In a small saucepan over medium heat, bring 2 tablespoons of the heavy cream to a simmer. Remove from the heat. Fold in the gelatin sheet, the remaining 2 tablespoons heavy cream, and the crème fraîche. Cover the pan with plastic wrap and set aside for 10 to 15 minutes.

3. In a medium bowl, combine the blanched potato, egg, chives, dill, capers, and the cooled cream mixture. Line a small 6 x 2-inch terrine mold with plastic wrap and fill it with the mixture. Cover the terrine with plastic wrap; the plastic should touch the surface. Refrigerate until it sets, 2 to 4 hours.

4. In a small bowl, combine the frisée with the olive oil and season with sea salt and pepper.

5. To serve, unmold the terrine and place it on a cutting board. Slice into 8 equal pieces. Garnish with slices of beet-cured salmon and the frisée salad. Option: Serve with a small side dish of pickled baby turnip, red onion, and gherkins.

CURED SALMON WITH SILKY GAZPACHO, AVOCADO & HERBS

This is another recipe that is perfect in summer, when tomatoes and other fresh herbs and vegetables are in season, vine-ripened, and often available locally. I specify the tomatoes in the recipe below, but more often than not you can adjust the recipe to the tomatoes that look best at your local farmers market. Feel free to use any fresh herbs you prefer.

SERVES 4 ✳ CURE TIME: 24 HOURS

CURED SALMON

2 tablespoons kosher salt

2 tablespoons granulated sugar

Zest of 1 lime

One 12-ounce skin-on, boneless loin-cut salmon fillet

GAZPACHO

2 large shallots

2 garlic cloves

3 medium ripe tomatoes, cored and coarsely chopped

2 red bell peppers, charred and peeled (see Notes, page 87), and seeded

1 poblano pepper, charred and peeled (see Notes, page 87), and seeded

2 cucumbers, peeled and coarsely chopped

¼ cup rice vinegar

½ cup extra-virgin olive oil

Juice of 1 lime, plus more as needed

Kosher salt

Freshly ground black pepper

---

2 avocados, halved, pitted, and cut into wedges, for garnish

10 ripe cherry tomatoes, halved, for garnish

Fresh herbs and blossoms, such as arugula flowers, for garnish

1. **For the cured salmon,** combine the salt, sugar, and lime zest in a small bowl. Place the salmon in a glass baking dish and rub the cure all over the salmon. Cover with plastic wrap. Refrigerate for 24 hours.

2. Once cured, remove the salmon and rinse under ice-cold running water to remove the cure. Pat dry with paper towels, wrap in plastic, and refrigerate until ready to serve.

3. **For the gazpacho,** place the shallots and garlic in a small microwave-safe bowl and microwave for 1 minute. Transfer to a blender with the tomatoes, peppers, cucumbers, and vinegar. Pulse until smooth.

4. With the blender running on medium speed, gradually add the olive oil and blend until the gazpacho is emulsified and smooth. Transfer the gazpacho to a bowl and season with lime juice, salt, and pepper, tasting and adjusting seasoning as needed.

5. To serve, remove the salmon from the refrigerator and use a sharp knife to thinly slice. You will need 12 to 16 slices. Spoon gazpacho into each of four serving bowls. Top each bowl with 3 to 4 slices salmon. Garnish with the avocado, cherry tomatoes, and herbs.

CURED
SALMON LOX, TOASTED FOCACCIA & GARLICKY TOMATO DRESSING

The word lox is derived from the Middle High German "lahs," meaning salmon. Lox is a fillet of salmon that has been gently cured in salt. For this preparation, a one-pound skin-on portion of salmon is gently cured in kosher salt seasoned with chopped fresh dill.

SERVES 4 ✳ CURE TIME: 24 HOURS

One 1-pound skin-on, boneless salmon fillet, preferably from head end

½ cup plus ½ teaspoon kosher salt

¼ cup chopped fresh dill

¼ cup cream cheese, at room temperature

¼ cup mayonnaise

1 teaspoon crushed cooked garlic (see Note)

½ teaspoon freshly ground black pepper

¼ cup Roma tomatoes, finely diced

1 teaspoon freshly squeezed lemon juice, plus more as needed

Four 3-by-3-inch squares focaccia, lightly toasted

¼ cup thinly sliced red onion

1. Prepare the lox by lining a shallow bowl or rimmed pan with plastic wrap. Place the salmon, skin side down, on the plastic wrap and spread the ½ cup salt and dill evenly over the salmon. Gently press the salt and dill into the salmon so it adheres. Cover with a second sheet of plastic wrap and place the salmon in the refrigerator to cure for 24 hours.

2. Once cured, unwrap the salmon and rinse under ice-cold running water to remove the cure. Pat dry with paper towels. Slice the salmon against the grain as thinly as possible—from the head end toward the tail end. Angle the knife so the blade slides along the inside surface of the skin once through the thick part of the fillet. Do not cut through the skin. Detach the slice from the skin using the knife and stack the slices as you continue to cut. You will need 8 to 12 slices.

3. In a medium bowl, whisk the cream cheese, mayonnaise, garlic, ½ teaspoon salt, and the pepper until smooth. Taste and adjust seasoning. Add the Roma tomatoes and lemon juice. Taste and adjust seasoning with additional lemon juice, salt, and pepper.

4. Halve the focaccia squares through the middle so you can make a sandwich. Spread some of the cream cheese mixture on the bottom piece of focaccia. Add a layer of 2 or 3 slices of the lox. Garnish with the sliced onion and cap with the focaccia top. Repeat for the remaining sandwiches and serve.

Note: To quickly cook garlic, put two or three cloves in a small microwave-safe bowl with 2 tablespoons extra-virgin olive oil. Cover with a paper towel and microwave until tender, 45 to 60 seconds.

CURED SALMON WITH CITRUS & SHAVED FENNEL

I love to serve this bright and delicious salad as a lunch option. Prepare all the ingredients ahead while the salmon is curing and then when the cured salmon is ready, assemble the dish right before enjoying it. The satsuma mandarin oranges are best between October and December, so this is usually an autumn dish in my household. If satsumas aren't available, you can use any type of orange. The recipe will still work.

SERVES 4 TO 6 ✳ CURE TIME: 24 HOURS

CURED SALMON

One 1 pound skin-on, boneless salmon fillet

¼ cup maple sugar or light brown sugar

¼ cup kosher salt

1 teaspoon powdered ginger

SALAD

1 small fennel bulb

¼ head frisée, core removed

1 mango, halved, peeled, pitted, and diced

¼ cup rice vinegar

¼ cup extra-virgin olive oil

Kosher salt and freshly ground black pepper

2 satsuma mandarin oranges, peeled and segmented

1 navel orange, peeled and segmented

1 pink grapefruit, peeled and segmented

Dill sprigs for garnish

1. **For the cured salmon,** place the salmon fillet skin side down on a baking sheet. In a small bowl, combine the maple sugar, salt, and ginger and sprinkle the mixture evenly over the salmon fillet, coating the entire surface. Cover the salmon with plastic wrap and refrigerate for 24 hours.

2. **For the salad,** set a mandoline to make paper-thin slices. Carefully shave the fennel bulb into a bowl. Rinse the fennel under ice-cold running water and refrigerate to chill for 15 minutes. Pick apart the frisée fronds and place in a bowl. Rinse thoroughly under ice-cold running water, drain, and refrigerate to chill for 15 minutes. Once the vegetables are chilled, combine them in a medium bowl with the mango and 2 tablespoons each of the vinegar and olive oil. Season with salt and pepper and toss together. Refrigerate until ready to serve.

3. In a medium bowl, combine the citrus segments along with the remaining 2 tablespoons vinegar and olive oil. Season with salt and pepper and toss gently to combine. Refrigerate until ready to serve.

4. Once ready to serve, rinse the salmon under ice-cold running water to remove the cure completely, then pat dry with paper towels. Place the salmon on a cutting board and, cutting at an angle, thinly slice starting at the head end of the fillet and continuing toward the tail. You will need 20 to 24 slices.

5. For each serving, layer 5 or 6 slices of salmon on a plate. Spoon the citrus and shaved fennel salad over the center of the slices. Garnish with dill sprigs or your favorite herbs. Serve chilled.

CURED

SALMON GRAVLAX TARTARE, LEMON AIOLI, ASIAN PEAR & NORI CRISPS

Salmon gravlax is the Scandinavian preparation of lox. Literally translated, gravlax is "salmon from the grave," which comes from the Middle Age preparation of salting the fish then burying it in the sand while it cured. Gravlax is similar to traditional lox, but it tastes more similar to sashimi. Gravlax is often cured with salt, sugar, citrus, fresh dill, black or white pepper, and, sometimes, aquavit, a Scandinavian alcohol distilled from potatoes. This cure recipe is one of my favorites and was passed down from a colleague who worked abroad in London.

SERVES 4 ✱ CURE TIME: 24 TO 48 HOURS

SALMON GRAVLAX

One 1-pound skinless, boneless side of salmon

6 whole cloves

2 star anise

1 teaspoon whole coriander seeds

1 teaspoon black peppercorns

½ cup kosher salt

¼ cup granulated sugar

Zest and juice of 1 lemon

Zest and juice of 1 lime

8 sprigs dill leaves, chopped, plus 12 dill fronds for garnish

LEMON AIOLI

½ cup olive oil

1 tablespoon champagne vinegar

2 tablespoons freshly squeezed lemon juice

1 teaspoon Dijon mustard

1 large egg yolk

¼ teaspoon kosher salt

CRISPY NORI

½ cup all-purpose flour

1 teaspoon kosher salt

½ cup cold sparkling water

¼ cup ice water

1 large egg, lightly beaten

Rapeseed oil for frying

2 nori sheets

---

2 Asian pears, cut into matchsticks

12 leaves red mizuna or arugula, rinsed

1. **For the salmon gravlax,** cut the salmon fillet in half. Dice half of the fillet into ¼-inch cubes until you have about 1 cup. Refrigerate the diced salmon, covered in plastic wrap, until ready to serve.

2. In a dry skillet over medium heat, toast the cloves, star anise, coriander seeds, and peppercorns until fragrant, 1 to 2 minutes. Let cool slightly. Transfer the toasted spices to a spice grinder and grind to a semi-coarse powder.

3. Transfer the spice powder to a medium bowl and add the salt, sugar, lemon and lime zests and juices, and chopped dill. Mix well.

4. Use a glass or ceramic nonreactive dish just large enough to hold the salmon fillet flat. Pour half of the cure mixture into the dish, spreading it evenly. Place the other salmon fillet onto the cure. Pack the remaining cure mixture evenly over the top surface of the salmon. Cover the dish tightly with plastic wrap. Refrigerate for at least 24 hours and up to 48 hours.

5. Rinse the salmon under ice-cold running water to remove the cure completely, then pat dry with paper towels. Dice the cured salmon into ¼-inch pieces (you need 1 cup). Tightly wrap any remaining gravlax in plastic wrap and refrigerate for up to 1 week.

6. **For the lemon aioli,** use a small food processor or blender to combine the olive oil, vinegar, lemon juice, mustard, egg yolk, and salt. Pulse or blend until the mixture is emulsified and thick. Transfer the aioli to a squeeze bottle or a small bowl and refrigerate until needed. You will use ¼ cup for the final dish. Store the remaining aioli in an airtight container for up to 1 week.

7. **For the crispy nori,** in a medium bowl stir together the flour and salt. Add the sparkling water, ice water, and egg. Stir with a fork just until combined—the batter should remain slightly lumpy. Do not overmix.

8. Pour rapeseed oil into a large, heavy-bottomed pot or Dutch oven to a depth of 1 to 2 inches. Heat the oil over medium-high heat until it reaches 375°F on a deep-fry or candy thermometer. Set a wire rack over paper towels for draining.

9. Working carefully near the hot oil, take 1 of the nori sheets and quickly coat it in the batter, allowing excess batter to drip off. Holding one corner, gently lower the battered nori sheet into the hot oil. Repeat immediately with the second nori sheet. Fry the nori sheets until crisp and lightly golden, 1 to 2 minutes per side. Use tongs or a spider skimmer to carefully remove the fried nori from the oil.

10. Transfer the fried nori to the wire rack and cool completely. Once cooled, gently break the fried nori sheets into approximately 20 bite-size crisps.

11. In a large bowl, combine the 1 cup reserved diced raw salmon and the 1 cup diced salmon gravlax. Add 1 tablespoon of the lemon aioli and gently stir to combine.

12. Divide the salmon tartare mixture among four serving plates. Attractively arrange the Asian pear sticks, and about 5 nori crisps, 3 dill fronds, and 3 mizuna leaves per plate around or alongside the tartare. Drizzle or dot each plate with the remaining 3 tablespoons lemon aioli. Serve immediately.

CURED

THAI-STYLE SALMON SASHIMI

Salmon is not a common ingredient in Thailand, but it has gained popularity in recent years. The results are a rapidly expanding number of spectacular recipes using traditional Thai techniques and flavor profiles while incorporating salmon. This recipe is a fusion of Japanese sashimi and a traditional Thai sauce.

SERVES 4 * CURE TIME: 30 MINUTES

One 1-pound sashimi-grade center-cut skinless, boneless salmon loin

½ teaspoon kosher salt

½ teaspoon plus 1 tablespoon granulated sugar

1 whole fresh Thai chili

2 cloves garlic, microwaved for 20 seconds

Juice of 2 lemons

¼ cup tamari

1 teaspoon fish sauce

1 teaspoon extra-virgin olive oil

1 teaspoon freshly ground black pepper

10 to 15 mint or basil leaves, garlic chips, and herb blossoms for garnish

1. Place the salmon in a shallow dish. In a small bowl combine the salt and the ½ teaspoon sugar. Dust the mixture over the salmon, coating both sides. Cover loosely with plastic wrap and refrigerate for 30 minutes to cure lightly.

2. In a blender, pulse the chili, garlic, lemon juice, tamari, fish sauce, olive oil, pepper, and the remaining 1 tablespoon sugar until smooth. Pour the sauce into a glass container and let rest for 20 minutes.

3. Place the salmon on a cutting board and slice into 16 thin pieces against the grain at a 90-degree angle, sashimi style. Set the pieces on a plate, cover with plastic wrap, and refrigerate until ready to serve.

4. To serve, strain the sauce through a fine-mesh sieve into a measuring cup. Put 3 to 4 tablespoons of the sauce into each of four bowls. Place 4 slices of the salmon into each bowl, garnish with the mint or basil leaves, garlic chips, and herb blossoms, and serve.

GRILLING

Grilling is a dry-cooking method that involves applying radiant heat to the surface of food, usually from below. It's a popular choice for its ability to create delicious smoky flavors and appealing grill marks. Grilling can occur using heat sources such as charcoal, gas, wood, or electricity. Each has its own set of strengths and weaknesses. I use wood, charcoal, and gas during the summer and a fantastic high-heat electric grill indoors during the winter. Grilling temperatures are usually high, so this technique requires constant vigilance and continuous monitoring. Thicker cuts work best and tend to hold up better to this more aggressive cooking technique.

HERE ARE SOME BASIC TIPS FOR GRILLING:

DRY THE FISH: Pat the salmon dry with paper towels before seasoning and cooking to increase the potential for browning.

SEASON THE FISH: At a minimum, use good-quality salt and pepper. If you have time, lightly cure the fish with salt (or a salt and sugar combination) and refrigerate for at least 30 minutes.

PREPARE THE GRILL: Heat the grill and lightly oil the grates to prevent sticking.

RUB WITH OIL: Use enough oil or fat to coat the fish. I use good-quality olive oil. Don't use too much oil or it will accelerate browning and increase the risk of burning.

DON'T MOVE THE FISH: Place the fish on the grill and leave it alone until the side that is in contact with the grill caramelizes, dries out a bit, and detaches from the grate. In other words, leave it alone until it has denatured enough to detach. Once the fish detaches, flip it and cook to 122°F for wild, 124°F for farmed, or to preference.

REMOVE THE FISH FROM THE GRILL: Once the desired temperature is reached, carefully remove the fish from the grill using a good spatula or a pair of metal tongs.

LET THE FISH REST: Let the fish rest for a few minutes on a plate, skin side up, before serving.

OPPOSITE: A salmon seiner motoring northwest through the Sitka Channel in Sitka, Alaska.

KALLISTE
58727

GRILLED SALMON WITH SUN-DRIED TOMATO & OLIVE VINAIGRETTE & SHISHITO PEPPERS

This recipe is bold in flavor but not so bold that it overpowers the flavor of the salmon. I prefer to use thick salmon portions. The sun-dried tomatoes, vinaigrette, and shishito peppers are the perfect balance to the salmon.

SERVES 4 ✳ COOK TO 122°F FOR WILD, 124°F FOR FARMED, OR TO DESIRED DONENESS

¼ cup extra-virgin olive oil, plus more for grill grates

¼ cup sun-dried tomatoes, diced

¼ cup diced Kalamata olives

¼ cup peeled, diced cucumber

1 tablespoon roughly chopped fresh thyme leaves

1 tablespoon roughly chopped fresh dill leaves

Juice of 2 lemons

2 teaspoons kosher salt, plus more to taste

1 teaspoon freshly ground black pepper, plus more to taste

One 1-pound skin-on, boneless salmon fillet, butterflied (see Note)

4 shishito peppers for garnish

Dill sprigs for garnish

Zest of 1 lemon for garnish

Fresh herbs such as sorrel for garnish

1. In a medium bowl, combine 3 tablespoons of the olive oil with the tomatoes, olives, cucumber, thyme, dill, and lemon juice. Season with some salt and pepper. Let the vinaigrette sit at room temperature while you make the salmon.

2. Preheat a gas grill to medium heat and oil the grill grates.

3. Season the salmon fillet with the 2 teaspoons salt and 1 teaspoon pepper. Drizzle the remaining 1 tablespoon olive oil over the fillet and coat both sides. Grill the salmon over medium heat, 4 to 5 minutes per side, until an instant-read thermometer inserted into the thickest part of a fillet is 122°F for wild, 124°F for farmed, or the fish is cooked to desired doneness. Rest the salmon on a plate, skin side up, for 3 to 4 minutes.

4. Meanwhile, place the shishito peppers on the grill, turning to char on all sides. (If your grill grates are wide, you may have to use a cast-iron skillet to char and cook the peppers or they will fall through the grates.) Transfer to a plate.

5. To serve, ladle the vinaigrette into a serving dish. Place the salmon fillet on the vinaigrette and garnish with the charred shishito peppers, dill sprigs, lemon zest, and fresh herbs. Serve family style, with a bowl of extra vinaigrette on the side.

Note: To butterfly a salmon fillet, lay the fillet flat on your cutting board, skin side down. Carefully slice down the center of the fillet lengthwise, almost to, but not through, the skin (about ½ inch from the skin). Gently open the fillet along this uncut portion, flattening it out like a book. This method yields a strong visual appeal and a more uniform thickness for consistent and even cooking.

GRILLED SALMON WITH HONEY-MUSTARD GLAZE

The first secret to this dish is a properly heated electric grill. I love using one during the colder months, so long as good ventilation is available. Mine is from Starfrit and it costs less than sixty dollars—I love it. The second trick is adding pickled jalapeño to the honey-mustard glaze. It really makes a difference.

SERVES 4 ✳ COOK TO 122°F FOR WILD, 124°F FOR FARMED, OR TO DESIRED DONENESS

GLAZE

¼ cup whole-grain mustard

2 tablespoons brown mustard

¼ cup honey

¾ cup plus 1 tablespoon low-sodium chicken broth

1 tablespoon diced pickled jalapeño pepper

1 teaspoon diced jalapeño pickling liquid

1 teaspoon cornstarch

Kosher salt and freshly ground black pepper

VEGETABLES

¼ cup extra-virgin olive oil, plus more for coating

1 pound russet potatoes, peeled and thinly sliced

1 leek, thinly sliced and sautéed in olive oil until tender

½ red pepper, thinly sliced and sautéed in olive oil until tender

Kosher salt and freshly ground black pepper

1 cup chicken broth

¼ pound maitake mushrooms, pulled into pieces

2 tablespoons minced shallot

¾ pound green beans, blanched and cut into ¼-inch pieces

SALMON

Four 3-ounce skin-on, boneless center-cut salmon fillets

Kosher salt and freshly ground black pepper

½ teaspoon paprika

1 tablespoon extra-virgin olive oil

1. **For the glaze,** combine the mustards, honey, ¾ cup broth, and diced jalapeño and pickling liquid in a small saucepan and bring to a simmer over medium heat. In a small bowl, combine the cornstarch with 1 tablespoon broth, stirring well, then add to the pot. Simmer until slightly thickened. Season with salt and pepper, remove from the heat, and set aside.

2. **For the vegetables,** preheat the oven to 350°F. Coat a small 6 x 8-inch baking dish with olive oil. Line the bottom of the dish with parchment paper to make removing the potatoes easier. In a large bowl, combine the potatoes, leeks, and red pepper and season with salt and black pepper. Layer the vegetable mixture in the baking dish, add the broth, and cover with foil. Bake until partially tender, about 20 minutes. Remove the foil and bake until fully cooked and golden brown, another 10 to 12 minutes. Let cool for 25 to 30 minutes, then transfer the vegetable mixture to a cutting board.

3. In a medium sauté pan over medium heat, add ¼ cup olive oil. Once shimmering, add the mushrooms and shallot. Sauté until golden brown and tender. Add the green beans and cook until heated through, 3 to 4 minutes. Remove from the heat and set aside.

4. **For the salmon,** preheat an electric grill to its highest setting (usually 450°F). Season the salmon with salt, pepper, and paprika. Coat the fillets with the olive oil.

5. Grill the salmon, skin side up, for 4 to 5 minutes. Flip and continue to cook the second side for 3 to 4 minutes, until an instant-read thermometer inserted into the thickest part of a fillet is 122°F for wild, 124°F for farmed, or the fish is cooked to desired doneness. Let the salmon rest on a plate, skin side up, for 3 to 4 minutes.

6. Cut the vegetable mixture into individual portions and place on four plates. Top with a skin side down salmon fillet. Spoon the mushrooms and beans around the salmon. Drizzle each plate with 2 to 3 tablespoons of the honey-mustard glaze before serving.

GRILLED SALMON WITH STRAWBERRY SALSA

I have been a member of a local farm CSA for nearly twenty years, and they have a fantastic strawberry patch where my family sources our strawberries each summer. This recipe was born one summer when we had an overabundance of fantastic strawberries and experimented with them in multiple ways (green, partially ripe, ripe, overripe, fresh, frozen, dried, and juiced). One evening, while creating a strawberry salsa, we added some spice—Merkén pepper from Chile—to the base and tried it on salmon. It was a home run. Merkén is similar to chipotle chili powder, but to me, it has a sweeter, almost fruity note that I prefer when paired with strawberries.

SERVES 4 ✳ COOK TO 122°F FOR WILD, 124°F FOR FARMED, OR TO DESIRED DONENESS

Four 4-ounce skin-on, boneless salmon fillets

1 teaspoon kosher salt, plus more to taste

1 teaspoon granulated sugar

1 pint fresh ripe strawberries, hulled and quartered

1 rib celery, minced

¼ cup rice vinegar

¼ cup plus 2 tablespoons extra-virgin olive oil, plus more for grill grates

Juice of 1 lemon

½ teaspoon Merkén pepper or chipotle chili powder

Freshly ground black pepper

1. Dust the salmon with the salt and sugar. Place on a plate, cover loosely with plastic wrap, and cure in the refrigerator for 1 hour.

2. In a medium bowl, combine the strawberries with the celery, vinegar, ¼ cup olive oil, lemon juice, and Merkén. Season with salt and pepper.

3. Preheat a gas grill to medium (or a charcoal grill until the coals are partially burned and glowing red).

4. Rinse the salmon with ice-cold running water, pat dry, and brush with the 2 tablespoons olive oil. Oil the grill grates. Place the salmon, skin side up, on the grates and grill until dark golden and lightly charred, 2 to 3 minutes. Turn the salmon skin side down and place slightly off to the side for indirect grilling, 4 to 5 minutes, until an instant-read thermometer inserted into the thickest part of a fillet is 122°F for wild, 124°F for farmed, or the fish is cooked to desired doneness. Rest the salmon on a plate, skin side up, for 3 to 4 minutes.

5. Serve family style, placing the salsa onto the platter and topping with salmon fillets skin side down. Optional: Garnish with edible flowers, mint leaves, and shaved scallion.

GRILLED

SALMON YAKITORI

I like to ask our fishmonger to save us a fresh salmon head for this recipe. Using a salmon head to make the yakitori glaze adds more gelatin, creating a stickier consistency that really adheres to the grilled fish strips and also assures complete utilization of the fish. If the head is unavailable, you can make the glaze without it. You can make more glaze than is called for in this recipe—store in an airtight container in the refrigerator for up to 1 week. It is absolutely delicious and great on any type of fish or chicken.

SERVES 4 ✳ COOK TO 122°F FOR WILD, 124°F FOR FARMED, OR TO DESIRED DONENESS

One 1-pound salmon head, gills removed, split in half nose to neck, and rinsed

3 green onions (scallions), whites cut into 3-inch lengths; greens sliced thin for serving

One 1-inch knob ginger, sliced in half

¾ cup sake, plus more to soak skewers

¾ cup mirin

6 tablespoons light brown sugar

¾ cup low-sodium soy sauce

One 1-pound skinless, boneless salmon belly, cut into 1-inch-wide by 3-inch-long strips

2 limes, cut into wedges, for serving

Red radishes, halved, for serving

2 tablespoons togarashi for serving

1. Heat a gas grill to medium heat or light a fire in a hibachi grill.

2. Place the salmon head, whites of the green onions, and ginger on a gas grill (you may need to use a cast-iron skillet on the grill) or hibachi and grill until lightly charred, about 3 minutes. Turn off the grill.

3. Transfer the grilled ingredients to a large pot and set over medium heat on the stovetop. Add the sake, mirin, and brown sugar and bring to a simmer. Simmer until the glaze is thick enough to fully coat the back of a spoon, 12 to 15 minutes. Once thickened, remove from the heat, stir in the soy sauce, and strain through a fine-mesh sieve into a clean bowl. Set the bowl over an ice bath to chill, then set aside.

4. Place the salmon strips in a zip-top bag. Pour the chilled yakitori glaze into the bag, seal, and allow to marinate in the refrigerator for 1 hour.

5. Meanwhile, soak eight wooden skewers in sake or water for at least 30 minutes.

6. Remove the salmon from the bag and pour the glaze into a bowl. Skewer each salmon strip with 2 skewers set slightly apart, which will keep the skewers from rolling while grilling.

7. Preheat a gas grill. Set one side of the grill to high, the other to low.

8. Grill the salmon skewers on the high heat side. As the salmon begins to char, brush with the reserved glaze and flip to continue cooking. Once the second side is slightly charred, brush with more glaze and shift the skewers to the cooler side of the grill. Finish grilling on the cool side of the grill until an instant-read thermometer inserted into the thickest part of a fillet is 122°F for wild, 124°F for farmed, or the fish is cooked to desired doneness. Transfer the skewers to a platter and allow to rest for 3 to 4 minutes.

9. To serve, place 2 skewers on a plate and top with sliced green onion, lime wedges, radishes, and a sprinkling of togarashi. Repeat for the remaining servings.

PAN-COOKING

PAN-SEARING & PAN-FRYING

Pan-cooking is a dry, high-heat cooking method used to create a flavorful brown crust on the surface of the fish. It's a quick process that involves cooking the food in a hot pan with a small amount of fat. I use a cast-iron skillet.

HERE ARE SOME BASIC TIPS FOR PAN-COOKING:

DRY THE FISH: Pat the salmon dry with paper towels before seasoning and cooking to increase the potential for browning.

SEASON THE FISH: At a minimum, use good-quality salt and pepper. If you have time, lightly cure the fish with salt (or a salt and sugar combination) and refrigerate for at least 30 minutes.

USE PROPER HEAT: A high-heat pan of 400°F is essential for successful pan-searing and a moderate heat of 350°F is needed for pan-frying. Proper heat assures the food will brown correctly and develop a rich, savory flavor. I prefer a large cast-iron skillet.

USE THE RIGHT AMOUNT OF FAT: For pan-searing, only a thin layer of oil or fat is needed to prevent sticking and promote even browning. If there is too much fat, enough to rise over the bottom edge of the salmon, you are no longer pan-searing but shallow frying. For pan-frying, a heavier amount of fat—usually one-half of the way up the side of the ingredient—is required.

DRY SURFACE: The surface of the food should be dry before it hits the pan. Excess moisture will create steam, inhibiting the browning process. Pat your food dry before cooking to improve the Maillard reaction.

DON'T OVERCROWD: Give the food enough space in the pan to ensure proper browning. Overcrowding will lower the pan's temperature and also lead to steaming instead of searing.

DON'T OVERCOOK: Salmon cooks quickly, so keep an eye on it. Insert an instant-read digital thermometer in the thickest part of the fillet and take a reading to determine if the fish is cooked (122°F for wild, 124°F for farmed, or to preference). The thickest part of the salmon will be opaque and flake easily with a fork.

LET THE FISH REST: Once the desired temperature is reached, remove the fish and let it rest for a few minutes on a plate, skin side up if there is skin.

USE THE RIGHT TOOL: Transfer the fish to a plate using a fish spatula or a metal spatula that is large enough to lift the fish without it breaking.

OPPOSITE: A freshwater salmon farm in Lake Llanquihue, off Playa Totoral Bajo, in Los Lagos, Chile.

PAN-SEARED SALMON WITH SPICY MAPO TOFU

Mápó dòufu (or tofu) is a Sichuan dish normally made with tofu and a spicy red sauce that includes tongue-numbing Sichuan peppercorns. For this recipe to reach its full flavor potential, it does require several somewhat unusual ingredients, but all are available online. The recipe is not that complicated, and the results are worth the effort. You can increase or decrease the level of spiciness to your taste. If you prefer to use just the sauce itself, you can eliminate the tofu. Either way, it tastes really good.

SERVES 4 ✳ COOK TO 122°F FOR WILD, 124°F FOR FARMED, OR TO DESIRED DONENESS

MAPO TOFU

2 cups low-sodium chicken broth

½ ounce dried shiitake mushrooms

12 scallions, cut into ½-inch lengths

1 package soft tofu, cut into ½-inch cubes

5 cloves garlic

One 3-inch knob ginger, peeled, cut into ¼-inch rounds, and lightly crushed

1 tablespoon gochugaru chili flakes

1 teaspoon Sichuan peppercorns, toasted and crushed

¼ cup broad bean chili paste

1 tablespoon fermented black beans

½ cup vegetable oil

½ cup oyster mushrooms, trimmed and chopped

2 tablespoons hoisin sauce

2 teaspoons toasted sesame oil

2 tablespoons tamari

1 tablespoon cornstarch

Kosher salt and freshly ground black pepper

Cayenne pepper

SALMON

1 tablespoon extra-virgin olive oil

Kosher salt and freshly ground black pepper

Four 4-ounce skin-on, boneless salmon fillets

---

4 cups steamed white rice for serving

Julienned summer squash (optional)

1. **For the mapo tofu,** heat the chicken broth in a medium saucepan over medium heat until simmering. Add the shiitake mushrooms and remove from the heat. Allow the mushrooms to soak until softened, 3 to 5 minutes. Use a slotted spoon to transfer the mushrooms to a cutting board. Once cool, chop fine and set aside.

2. Place the scallions and tofu into the saucepan with the mushroom-infused chicken broth and bring to a simmer over medium heat. Simmer for 2 to 3 minutes, then remove from the heat.

3. In the bowl of a food processor fitted with the metal blade, add the garlic, ginger, chili flakes, peppercorns, chili paste, black beans, and 6 tablespoons of the vegetable oil. Process until a paste forms, 60 to 90 seconds. Transfer this spicy bean paste to a bowl and set aside.

4. Heat the remaining 2 tablespoons vegetable oil in large sauté pan over medium heat and add the reserved shiitakes and chopped oyster mushrooms. Sauté until the mushrooms are tender, about 5 minutes. Add the spicy bean paste and continue to cook for 2 to 3 minutes. Add the mushroom-infused chicken broth with scallions and tofu and simmer for 1 to 2 minutes. Stir in the hoisin sauce and sesame oil and continue simmering for 2 minutes.

5. In a small bowl, combine the tamari and cornstarch, stirring until the cornstarch dissolves. Add the slurry to the pan and stir until the mixture thickens. Season with salt, pepper, and cayenne, tasting and adjusting as needed. Remove from the heat.

6. **For the salmon,** heat the olive oil in a large cast-iron skillet over medium heat. Season both sides of the salmon with salt and pepper and place skin side down in the pan. Allow the skin to brown, 2 to 3 minutes. Carefully flip the salmon and cook

for about 1 minute more, until an instant-read thermometer inserted into the thickest part of a fillet is 122°F for wild, 124°F for farmed, or the fish is cooked to desired doneness. Rest the salmon on a plate, skin side up, for a few minutes.

7. To serve, place a scoop of rice onto each of four plates. Top with julienned summer squash, if desired, and the seared salmon, skin side up. Spoon the mapo tofu over the salmon and serve hot.

PAN-SEARED
SALMON BURGER WITH SAUERKRAUT & WASABI RUSSIAN DRESSING

This recipe is delicious. The smoked salmon added to the burger mixture is the secret, and the wasabi adds a nice kick to the dressing. Hot pepper sauce makes a good substitute if you can't find wasabi. I use a stainless steel ring mold to shape the burger while cooking it in a cast-iron skillet. Salmon burgers are my favorite quick, easy, and healthy weeknight meal, and they are wonderful year-round.

SERVES 4 * COOK TO 122°F FOR WILD, 124°F FOR FARMED, OR TO DESIRED DONENESS

One 12-ounce skinless, boneless salmon fillet

4 ounces store-bought smoked salmon

2 large egg yolks

1 teaspoon kosher salt

½ teaspoon freshly ground black pepper

2 tablespoons extra-virgin olive oil

½ cup Russian dressing

¼ teaspoon prepared wasabi

4 pretzel buns, toasted

½ cup prepared sauerkraut

4 small dill pickles or gherkins

1. On a cutting board, slice the salmon fillet and smoked salmon into strips and then into cubes, roughly chopping until the pieces are approximately ¼ inch in size. Keep randomly chopping the fresh and smoked salmon on your cutting board to further reduce the size of the chunks. The cuts do not have to be perfect—the goal is to create a range of small and large pieces. Place the chopped salmon in an ice-cold bowl or in a bowl set over ice.

2. Add the egg yolks to the salmon and stir vigorously using a metal spoon until the mixture starts to stick together. Season with the salt and pepper. Stir a few more times. The salmon should stick together as it starts to emulsify.

3. Heat the olive oil in a cast-iron skillet set over medium heat. Place 4 (3-inch-diameter) metal ring molds into the pan and fill the molds with the salmon mixture. Each should be around 3½ to 4 ounces in size. If you don't have metal ring molds, form 4 even-size patties with your hands and place them in the pan. Cook until golden brown, about 5 minutes. Use a small spatula to carefully flip the burgers, and continue to cook until the second side is golden brown, about 4 minutes.

4. In a small bowl, combine the Russian dressing and wasabi, stirring until thoroughly combined.

5. To serve, spread the Russian dressing mixture over the surface of the bottoms and tops of each bun. Place the salmon patties on the bottom buns. Top each patty with 2 tablespoons sauerkraut (or serve it on the side), then cover with the top buns. Serve with a pickle on the side.

PAN-SEARED

SALMON TTEOKBOKKI

Tteokbokki is a chunky little tubular rice cake (*tteok*) that is stir-fried (*bokki*) and tossed with a delicious sauce. You can find the tteok at many Asian markets, but my favorite is from an online source, Harmony Global Foods. For kelp and seaweed, I have tried nearly a dozen sources and prefer Maine Coast Sea Vegetables. The products, which can be purchased online and often at Whole Foods, are fantastic and regularly tested for purity.

SERVES 4 ✻ COOK TO 122°F FOR WILD, 124°F FOR FARMED, OR TO DESIRED DONENESS

½ cup gochujang

1 tablespoon gochugaru

1 tablespoon honey powder or granulated sugar

One 8-inch piece dried sugar kelp

¼ cup fish sauce

1 pound tteok

½ cup finely sliced scallion, plus more for garnish

1 large peeled carrot, cut into matchsticks

1 small peeled daikon radish, cut into matchsticks

1 tablespoon extra-virgin olive oil

Four 4-ounce skin-on, boneless salmon fillets

Kosher salt and freshly ground black pepper

1 tablespoon toasted sesame seeds

1. In a small bowl, combine the gochujang, gochugaru, and honey powder and set aside.

2. Place the sugar kelp in a medium saucepan with 3 cups water and the fish sauce. Bring to a simmer over medium heat and continue simmering for 15 minutes. Use a slotted spoon to remove and discard the kelp.

3. Add the tteok to the saucepan, then add the gochujang mixture and the ½ cup scallion. Return to a simmer over medium heat, stirring occasionally, until the mixture thickens and the rice cakes become tender, 10 to 12 minutes. The cakes will be thick and shiny. Stir in the carrot and radish. Remove from the heat and set aside, covered, to allow the carrot and radish to wilt.

4. In a large cast-iron skillet, heat the olive oil over medium heat. Season both sides of the salmon with salt and pepper. Place the salmon skin side down in the pan and cook until browned, 2 to 3 minutes. Flip the salmon and cook about 1 minute more, until an instant-read thermometer inserted into the thickest part of a fillet is 122°F for wild, 124°F for farmed, or the fish is cooked to desired doneness. Rest the salmon on a plate, skin side up, for a few minutes.

5. To serve, portion out about ½ cup of the tteokbokki and sauce into each of four serving bowls. Top each with a salmon fillet. Garnish with the sesame seeds and scallion. Drizzle any remaining tteokbokki sauce over the salmon and serve.

PAN-SEARED SALMON WITH KALE-CASHEW PESTO

Half of my family is from Central America, and we have a small *finca*, or farm, close to the Pacific Ocean where we grow lots of fruits, vegetables, and nuts, including cashews. Every April, our cashew (or *marañón*) trees bear fruit and the bounty is plentiful. This recipe was developed while visiting the farm during cashew season. Delicious salmon is widely available locally. If desired, serve with roasted butternut squash, carrots, and red cabbage.

SERVES 4 ✳ COOK TO 122°F FOR WILD, 124°F FOR FARMED, OR TO DESIRED DONENESS

KALE-CASHEW PESTO

Kosher salt

2½ ounces baby kale (roughly one-half of a clamshell)

½ cup roasted cashews

½ cup roasted pistachios

½ cup basil leaves

½ cup extra-virgin olive oil

¼ cup rice vinegar

Freshly ground black pepper

SALMON

Four 4-ounce skinless, boneless salmon fillets, at least 2 inches thick, butterflied (see Note)

3 tablespoons extra-virgin olive oil

1 clove garlic, minced

1 teaspoon chopped flat-leaf parsley leaves

1 teaspoon kosher salt

1 teaspoon agave powder

1. **For the kale-cashew pesto,** bring a large pot of salted water to a boil. Add the kale and blanch for 1 minute. Transfer to a blender. Blanch the cashews and pistachios for 1 minute, then use a small metal skimmer to fish them out; add them to the blender. Add the basil leaves to the blender (no need to blanch) and ¼ cup of the blanching liquid. Pulse until the mixture starts to blend. With the blender running, gradually add the olive oil until fully incorporated. Add the vinegar and blend on high speed for 1 minute. Season with salt and pepper. The finished pesto should be mostly smooth with some tiny pieces of the nuts for texture. Transfer the kale-cashew pesto to a bowl and reserve.

2. **For the salmon,** place the fillets on a plate. In a small bowl, combine 2 tablespoons of the olive oil, garlic, parsley, salt, and agave and pour over the fillets. Allow the fillets to marinate, refrigerated, for 30 minutes.

3. Remove the fillets from the marinade and pat them dry. Heat the remaining 1 tablespoon olive oil in a large cast-iron skillet over medium heat until just shy of the smoke point (the oil will be shimmering and radiating heat). Place the salmon split side up (flat side down) and press gently to start the searing process. Allow the salmon to cook until golden brown, 2 to 3 minutes, then gently flip to cook the other side. Continue cooking for 3 to 4 minutes, until an instant-read thermometer inserted into the thickest part of a fillet is 122°F for wild, 124°F for farmed, or the fish is cooked to desired doneness.

4. Use a fish spatula to remove each fillet from the pan and place on each of four plates, flat side up. Drizzle with the kale-cashew pesto. Serve at once.

Note: To butterfly a skinless salmon fillet, lay the fillet flat on your cutting board, skin side down. Carefully slice down the center of the fillet lengthwise, about ½ inch from the cutting board. Gently open the fillet along this uncut portion, flattening it out like a book. The result is a fillet that, when folded, is identical on both sides. This method yields a strong visual appeal and a more uniform thickness for consistency and even cooking.

PAN-SEARED SALMON WITH SPICY UDON NOODLES

Though this recipe calls for salmon, you can use any type of fish. Ask your local fishmonger or the attendant at your supermarket seafood department to portion out a center-cut loin of salmon. Thick fillets work best for this preparation, so the fish will be slightly undercooked when it is served.

SERVES 4 ✳ COOK TO 122°F FOR WILD, 124°F FOR FARMED, OR TO DESIRED DONENESS

Kosher salt

2 tablespoons extra-virgin olive oil

6 ounces fresh shiitake mushrooms, stems removed, sliced ¼ inch thick

2 cloves garlic, minced

One 2-inch knob ginger, peeled and minced

1 cup low-sodium chicken or vegetable broth

⅓ cup rice vinegar

¼ cup low-sodium soy sauce

1 tablespoon molasses

½ ounce dried shiitake mushrooms, soaked in warm water to soften, stems discarded, and minced

1 tablespoon chili garlic crunch

Four 4-ounce skin-on, boneless salmon fillets

Freshly ground black pepper

1 pound fresh udon noodles

1 tablespoon togarashi

Carrot julienne, and corn kernels, for garnish (optional)

1. Bring a large pot of salted water to a boil.

2. In a medium saucepan, heat 1 tablespoon of the olive oil over medium heat. Add the fresh shiitakes, garlic, and ginger, and gently sauté until softened and fragrant, 2 to 3 minutes. Add the broth, vinegar, soy sauce, molasses, and reconstituted shiitakes and simmer until slightly reduced, 6 to 8 minutes. Stir in the chili garlic crunch and reserve on the stovetop.

3. Heat the remaining 1 tablespoon olive oil in a large cast-iron skillet over medium heat. Season both sides of the salmon fillets with salt and pepper and place skin side up in the skillet. Brown for 3 minutes, then flip the salmon and cook 2 minutes more. (The fish will be barely cooked in the middle. If you prefer a fully cooked fish, add 2 to 3 minutes more to the cook time.) Rest the salmon on a plate, skin side up.

4. Once the water is boiling, add the udon noodles. Cook for 1 minute. Use a pasta spoon to transfer the cooked noodles to the saucepan with the broth and stir to combine. Turn the heat to medium and gently simmer until the broth thickens slightly, 2 to 3 minutes.

5. To serve, slice each salmon fillet in half. Portion the noodles and some of the broth into four bowls. Top each bowl of noodles with 2 salmon halves and garnish with a dusting of togarashi. Add carrots, zucchini, and corn, if using.

PAN-SEARED SALMON WITH PASTA & PESTO

As you might have guessed, I love pairing different types of pesto with salmon. Pesto's herbaceous base and oil and seasoning components make for a good combination. Plus, the oil in the pesto helps to caramelize the fish.

SERVES 4 ✳ COOK TO 122°F FOR WILD, 124°F FOR FARMED, OR TO DESIRED DONENESS

Four 3-ounce skin-on, boneless salmon fillets

Kosher salt and freshly ground black pepper

4 ounces penne pasta

½ cup jarred pesto

2 tablespoons extra-virgin olive oil

½ cup halved mixed cherry tomatoes

2 ounces salad greens

Grated Parmesan for serving (optional)

1. Season the salmon with salt and pepper and set aside.

2. Bring a large pot of salted water to a boil. Cook the pasta according to package directions. Drain the pasta and transfer to a large bowl. Add ¼ cup of the pesto and toss to coat.

3. In a medium cast-iron skillet, heat the olive oil over medium heat. Add the salmon fillets, skin side down. Cook for 4 minutes, then flip the fillets and continue cooking for 3 to 4 more minutes, until an instant-read thermometer inserted into the thickest part of a fillet is 122°F for wild, 124°F for farmed, or the fish is cooked to desired doneness. Rest the salmon on a plate, skin side up, until ready to serve.

4. Return the skillet to medium heat and add the tomatoes and greens. Add the remaining ¼ cup pesto and stir until the vegetables wilt, about 3 minutes. Transfer the tomatoes and greens to the bowl with the pasta and gently stir. Taste and season with salt and pepper as needed.

5. To serve, divide the pasta among four serving plates. Place the salmon fillets skin side up on top of the pasta. Sprinkle with Parmesan, if using.

PAN-SEARED SALMON WITH KOHLRABI & RADISH SALAD

During autumn, my local CSA loads me up with kohlrabi, which triggers an exploration of usage and flavor matching. The flavor of the kohlrabi lends itself to salmon and has a texture similar to raw jicama when peeled. Though this is made with raw kohlrabi, if you prefer a warm salad, you can heat the salad in the microwave for 30 to 45 seconds after it has marinated in the refrigerator.

SERVES 4 ✳ COOK TO 122°F FOR WILD, 124°F FOR FARMED, OR TO DESIRED DONENESS

1 cup julienned kohlrabi

½ cup peeled and julienned daikon radish

½ cup julienned carrot

1 medium shallot, minced

1 small bunch fresh dill, lightly chopped, 3 to 4 sprigs reserved for garnish

⅓ cup plus 1 tablespoon extra-virgin olive oil

¼ cup rice vinegar

1 teaspoon Dijon mustard

Kosher salt and freshly ground black pepper

Four 4-ounce skin-on or skinless, boneless salmon fillets

1 teaspoon cornstarch

Edible flowers, for serving (optional)

1. In a medium bowl, combine the kohlrabi, daikon, and carrot. Add the shallots, 1 heaping tablespoon of the chopped dill, ⅓ cup of the olive oil, vinegar, and mustard. Toss together. Season with salt and pepper. Refrigerate the salad for 20 to 30 minutes.

2. Season the salmon fillets with salt and pepper, and sprinkle the cornstarch over the fillets.

3. Heat 1 tablespoon olive oil in a large cast-iron skillet over medium-high heat. Place the salmon in the pan skin side up. Cook for 4 minutes. Flip the fillets and continue to cook until lightly browned, 3 to 4 minutes, and an instant-read thermometer inserted into the thickest part of a fillet is 122°F for wild, 124°F for farmed, or the fish is cooked to desired doneness. Rest the salmon on a plate, skin side up, for a few minutes. Slice each fillet into several pieces.

4. To serve, divide the salad among four plates. Surround the salad with salmon pieces and garnish with dill sprigs. Optional: Top with edible flowers (We used citrus begonia flowers in the photo.).

PAN-SEARED SALMON WITH BOULANGÈRE POTATOES & LEEKS

Though salmon is new to many of the cultures that inform the recipes in this book, this is not the case when it comes to classic French cookery and items like boulangère-prepared potatoes. The French have a long history of working with salmon, and many classic French recipes pair well with it. When it comes to boulangère potatoes, Yukon golds work best, and I love serving them with leeks in a further nod to classic French cooking. Leeks are high in vitamins A, C, and K, and beautifully complement the taste of salmon.

SERVES 4 ✻ COOK TO 122°F FOR WILD, 124°F FOR FARMED, OR TO DESIRED DONENESS

2 tablespoons extra-virgin olive oil, plus more for coating

2 pounds Yukon gold potatoes, peeled and sliced ⅛ inch thick

1 tablespoon chopped fresh rosemary leaves

Kosher salt and freshly ground black pepper

1 cup low-sodium chicken broth

1 large leek

2 tablespoons rice vinegar

1 tablespoon minced fresh basil

1 tablespoon minced garlic

¼ teaspoon red pepper flakes

Four 4-ounce skin-on, boneless salmon-loin fillets

Arugula sprouts for garnish

1. Preheat the oven to 350°F.

2. Lightly coat a 6 x 9-inch glass baking dish with olive oil. To make the potato casserole, start with a layer of sliced potato, then a sprinkling of rosemary, 1 teaspoon salt, and 1 teaspoon pepper. Then add another layer of potatoes, rosemary, salt, and pepper. Keep going until all the potatoes are used up. Pour the broth over the potatoes. Cover with aluminum foil and bake for 25 minutes. Remove the foil and bake until the potatoes are golden brown, another 10 minutes. Remove from the oven and cool for 15 minutes. Transfer the potatoes from the baking dish to a cutting board.

3. Trim all but 1 inch of the leek greens. Peel the outer layer of the white part of the leek and rinse the remaining leek, ensuring any dirt caught in the center is loosened and removed. Slice the leek into ½-inch rings. Place the rings flat side down in a small sauté pan with ¼ cup water, the vinegar, basil, garlic, and red pepper flakes. Cover the pan and heat on medium until gently steaming. Reduce the heat to low and cook until the leek is tender, 15 to 20 minutes. Lightly season with salt and pepper.

4. Meanwhile, season the salmon fillets all over with salt and pepper and let rest at room temperature for 20 minutes.

5. Place a large cast-iron skillet over medium heat. Add 2 tablespoons olive oil and place the salmon skin side down in the pan. Cook until browned, 4 to 5 minutes. Flip and cook 3 to 4 minutes more, until an instant-read thermometer inserted into the thickest part of a fillet is 122°F for wild, 124°F for farmed, or the fish is cooked to desired doneness. Rest the salmon on a plate, skin side up, for 3 to 4 minutes.

6. To serve, cut the potatoes into individual portions. Place the potatoes onto each of four serving plates and garnish with arugula sprouts. Divide the leek rings among the plates, placing them around the perimeter. Drizzle with a little of the liquid from the pan. Place the salmon fillets on top of the potatoes and serve.

PAN-SEARED

MAPLE-BOURBON GLAZED SALMON

I first created this recipe back in 1993. I was a consultant to a major seafood-processing company, which was successful in selling a version of the dish to a then-emerging retail club store out of Washington State that has since become a household name. More than thirty years later, I continue to find versions at the fresh seafood case at various retailers. Let's agree: It's a popular flavor combination for salmon, and it's easy to prepare.

SERVES 4 * COOK TO 122°F FOR WILD, 124°F FOR FARMED, OR TO DESIRED DONENESS

Four 3-ounce skinless, boneless salmon fillets

Kosher salt and freshly ground black pepper

5 tablespoons unsalted butter, chilled

¼ cup bourbon whiskey

½ cup maple syrup

Finely chopped chives (optional)

1. Season the salmon fillets with salt and pepper.

2. Melt 1 tablespoon of the butter in a medium cast-iron skillet over medium heat. Place 1 salmon fillet in the pan and cook for 5 minutes per side, carefully brushing each side with the butter in the pan as it cooks. (Cook until an instant-read thermometer inserted into the thickest part of a fillet is 122°F for wild, 124°F for farmed, or the fish is cooked to desired doneness.) Transfer to a plate and repeat, using 1 tablespoon butter with each fillet.

3. Remove the pan from the heat and add the bourbon, swirling carefully. Return the pan to medium-low heat and simmer until the bourbon has reduced slightly. Be very careful as bourbon can ignite over an open flame. Stir in the maple syrup and the remaining 1 tablespoon butter. Stir, then remove from the heat. Add the chives, if using. Gently swirl the pan until the butter has melted. Taste and season with salt and pepper as needed.

4. To serve, spoon 2 tablespoons sauce onto each plate and set the salmon fillets on the sauce. Optional: Garnish with emerald crystal lettuce.

PAN-SEARED
SALMON WITH ALMOND & CELERY ROOT SKORDALIA & ROASTED BRUSSELS SPROUTS

Skordalia, a puree of garlic in a base of nuts, potatoes, or bread, is of Greek origin. It competes directly with hummus and is, in my opinion, equally delicious. Yet few people know of it or prepare it at home. It is delicious enough to try. I switch it up by using a base of organic almonds and root vegetables like celery root, parsnip, or carrots, which are readily available in New England, where I live. The skordalia is super creamy and pairs well with both fresh and smoked salmon.

SERVES 4 * COOK TO 122°F FOR WILD, 124°F FOR FARMED, OR TO DESIRED DONENESS

Four 4-ounce skin-on, boneless salmon fillets

Kosher salt

1 teaspoon Aleppo pepper powder, plus more for sprinkling

¾ cup extra-virgin olive oil, plus more as needed

1 pound celery root, peeled and cut into 8 equal pieces

1 yellow onion, quartered

2 cloves garlic

½ cup raw almonds

½ bunch cilantro

¼ cup freshly squeezed lemon juice

Freshly ground black pepper

1 pound brussels sprouts, trimmed and halved

2 tablespoons honey

2 tablespoons rose harissa

½ teaspoon Maldon flaky sea salt

1. Preheat the oven to 425°F.

2. Place the salmon on a plate. Season all over with kosher salt and Aleppo pepper powder. Coat the fillets with 2 tablespoons olive oil and refrigerate for 15 minutes.

3. Bring a medium saucepan of salted water to a boil and add the celery root, onion, and garlic. Simmer over medium heat until the celery root is tender, 10 to 12 minutes. A knife inserted into the celery root should slide in with little resistance. Remove from the heat and add the almonds. Let steep for 5 minutes.

4. Strain the celery root, onion, garlic, and almonds through a fine-mesh sieve into a large measuring cup. Transfer the vegetables and nuts to a blender and pulse, adding 1 or 2 tablespoons of the reserved water at a time, until the mixture starts to churn smoothly.

5. Add the cilantro, ¼ cup of the olive oil, and the lemon juice and blend until smooth, adding more poaching water and olive oil until the skordalia is smooth and creamy. Season with salt and pepper. Transfer to an airtight container and refrigerate until ready to use (you will have leftover skordalia to enjoy).

6. In a large bowl, toss the brussels sprouts with the honey, rose harissa, and ¼ cup olive oil. Toss until evenly coated and place on a baking sheet. Roast in the oven until lightly charred and tender, 10 to 12 minutes.

7. Meanwhile, heat the remaining 2 tablespoons olive oil in a large cast-iron skillet over medium heat. Place the salmon fillets in the skillet, skin side down, and cook until the skin is browned, about 4 minutes. Flip the fillets and cook 2 to 3 minutes more, until an instant-read thermometer inserted into the thickest part of a fillet is 122°F for wild, 124°F for farmed, or the fish is cooked to desired doneness. Rest the salmon on a plate, skin side up, for 3 to 4 minutes.

8. To serve, sprinkle the salmon with the flaky sea salt and Aleppo pepper powder. Transfer the fillets to each of four plates, adding dollops of the skordalia and some of the brussels sprouts. Optional: Garnish with pink-tipped parsley.

PAN-SEARED SALMON BURGER WITH PICKLED LEMON

This salmon burger is a healthy and delicious summer alternative to a traditional red-meat option. The sriracha mayonnaise and pickled lemon add vibrance and complexity, resulting in a mildly spicy and very craveable bite. Fattier salmon works best when making burgers. You can serve this with a side of pickled carrots and daikon radish.

SERVES 4

- **⅓ cup mayonnaise**
- **2 tablespoons sriracha**
- **One 12-ounce skinless, boneless salmon belly fillet**
- **2 large egg yolks**
- **½ teaspoon kosher salt**
- **½ teaspoon freshly ground black pepper**
- **4 potato buns**
- **Pickled Lemon (recipe follows)**
- **¼ cup thinly sliced red onion**

1. In a small bowl, combine the mayonnaise with the sriracha and refrigerate, covered, until ready to use.

2. On a cutting board, cut the salmon into ¼-inch cubes and then continue to chop until the salmon is fine in texture. Place the chopped salmon in an ice-cold bowl or in a bowl set over ice. Add the egg yolks and salt and pepper and mix by hand until it just comes together; do not overmix.

3. Using your hands or a round mold, shape the salmon mixture into four equal-size patties.

4. Heat a large cast-iron skillet coated with cooking spray over medium-high heat. Place the patties in the skillet and cook until golden brown, about 3 minutes per side. Transfer the patties to a plate and set aside.

5. Wipe the skillet clean, reduce the heat to medium, and place the potato bun halves cut sides down in the pan. (You may need to do this in batches.) Toast until golden, 2 to 3 minutes. Transfer the buns to a cutting board.

6. To assemble, spread a spoonful of the spicy mayo on the bottom buns, then top with the salmon patties, pickled lemon, red onion, and top buns.

PICKLED LEMON

MAKES ABOUT ½ CUP

- **½ cup distilled white vinegar**
- **¼ cup granulated sugar**
- **½ teaspoon kosher salt**
- **2 lemons, very thinly sliced, seeds removed**

In a medium bowl, combine ½ cup water with the vinegar, sugar, and salt and stir until the sugar dissolves. Place the lemon slices in the brine and soak in the refrigerator for at least 2 hours and preferably up to 24 hours. Store the pickled lemons in an airtight container in the refrigerator for up to 1 week.

PAN-SEARED
TAJIN-SEASONED SALMON OPEN-FACE SANDWICHES

I constantly search out and experiment with new flavors that might be complementary with salmon. It was obvious when I first tried Mexican Tajin seasoning that there was such a match with salmon. The key ingredient in the seasoning that makes the match possible is the dehydrated powdered lime, though the complexity of the guajillo, pasilla, and chile de árbol add wonderful complexity, too. The origin of this recipe was a mental image of how the flavors would pair.

SERVES 4

1 bunch cilantro

¼ cup pine nuts, toasted

1 clove garlic

½ cup extra-virgin olive oil

¼ cup freshly squeezed lime juice

Kosher salt and freshly ground black pepper

2 carrots, peeled and shaved thin on a mandoline

½ head of fennel, cored and shaved thin on a mandoline

1 jalapeño pepper, seeded, finely diced

2 tablespoons rice vinegar

One 12-ounce skinless, boneless salmon fillet, cut against the grain into 24 to 32 (½-inch) slices

1 teaspoon Tajin seasoning

2 radishes, thinly sliced

4 center-cut slices whole-grain French boule, toasted

1 cup baby salad greens

1. In a blender, pulse the cilantro, pine nuts, garlic, ¼ cup olive oil, and lime juice until smooth. Season with salt and pepper. Transfer the cilantro pesto to an airtight container and refrigerate until ready to plate the dish.

2. Heat 2 tablespoons of the olive oil in a medium sauté pan set over medium heat. Add the carrots, fennel, and jalapeño and sauté until tender, 2 to 3 minutes. Cover the pan and turn off the heat but leave the pan on the burner until the vegetables are cool. Stir in the vinegar. Taste and add salt and pepper as needed.

3. Season the salmon all over with the Tajin and coat with the remaining 2 tablespoons olive oil. Place a large cast-iron skillet over medium heat and spray lightly with cooking spray. Once the pan is hot, place the individual salmon slices flat in the pan (you will need to work in batches). Cook until the salmon slices are browned and fully cooked, flipping once, about 4 minutes. Repeat for the remaining slices.

4. Season the radishes with salt and pepper. Place the toasted bread on each of four plates. Divide the greens among the slices of bread, then the radishes. Drizzle the cilantro pesto over the carrot-fennel slaw. Top the slaw with 6 to 8 overlapping slices of salmon. Spoon additional fennel slaw on the plate and serve.

PAN-FRIED

SPICED SALMON LOIN WITH DAIKON & CUCUMBER RELISH

The inspiration for this dish came from a dining experience in Tokyo while researching this book. I use *togarashi* (the Japanese word for chili pepper), which can be found online. Shichimi togarashi is my favorite and includes tingly and numbing sansho peppercorns. It has been around for hundreds of years in Japan. It's very popular in Nagano and Kyoto, where you can find it in spice shops. Here in the US, you can find it online. Use sashimi-grade salmon loin that has been deep frozen to reduce the risk of foodborne illness.

SERVES 4

SPICED SALMON LOIN

½ sheet nori, crumbled into small pieces

1 tablespoon dried orange peel

1 tablespoon Hondashi powder (Japanese stock base)

1 teaspoon sesame seed

1 teaspoon ground ginger

½ teaspoon ground red pepper flakes

½ teaspoon sansho pepper powder

One 1-pound skinless, boneless salmon loin

1 cup extra-virgin olive oil

GINGER SAUCE

½ cup fresh orange or yuzu juice

½ cup tamari

2 teaspoons grated ginger

1 teaspoon grated garlic

1 teaspoon shichimi togarashi powder

CHILI OIL

¼ cup extra-virgin olive oil

1 tablespoon paprika

DAIKON-CUCUMBER RELISH

¼ cup peeled and finely diced daikon radish

¼ cup finely diced Japanese cucumber

1 tablespoon rice vinegar

1 tablespoon mirin

1 tablespoon low-sodium soy sauce

---

24 thin slices baby cucumber for serving

1 tablespoon edible flowers, such as starflower, for garnish (optional)

1. **For the spiced salmon loin,** combine the nori, orange peel, Hondashi powder, sesame seed, ginger, pepper flakes, and sansho pepper in a small bowl. Trim the salmon to a length of 14 inches long by 2½ inches wide. Place the salmon in a baking dish and dust with the spice mix, rolling and gently rubbing until evenly coated. Refrigerate until ready to cook.

2. Pour the olive oil into a large cast-iron skillet and heat to 350°F on an instant-read thermometer. Carefully set the salmon in the oil and allow to cook until evenly browned on all sides, 1 to 2 minutes per side. The salmon will be just cooked on the outside but raw in the middle. Use a large spatula to transfer the salmon to a large plate. Set aside until ready to serve.

3. **For the ginger sauce,** whisk all ingredients in a medium bowl until incorporated. (The sauce can be made in advance, stored in an airtight container in the refrigerator, for up to 1 week.)

4. **For the chili oil,** slightly warm the olive oil in a small saucepan over low heat. Transfer to a small bowl and stir in the paprika. Set aside.

5. **For the daikon-cucumber relish,** combine all ingredients in a small bowl.

6. To serve, slice the salmon into 24 thin slices. On each of four plates, place 6 slices of the salmon. Pour a generous amount of the ginger sauce around the salmon and drizzle the chili oil over the sauce. Top each slice of salmon with a thin slice of cucumber and some of the daikon-cucumber relish. Garnish with edible flowers, if using.

PAN-FRIED SALMON WITH LEMONY BROCCOLI RABE

Consistent with other recipes in this book, this one leverages a boldly flavored ingredient, broccoli rabe, to balance the flavor of the salmon. Both are available year-round, and I find the quality of properly thawed frozen salmon perfect for this preparation. If using previously frozen fish, be sure to lightly cure it first. If fresh, a simple coating of salt and pepper before cooking works well.

SERVES 4 ✳ COOK TO 122°F FOR WILD, 124°F FOR FARMED, OR TO DESIRED DONENESS

Four 3-ounce skin-on, boneless center-cut salmon fillets

Kosher salt and freshly ground black pepper

½ cup extra-virgin olive oil, plus more for drizzling

1 pound broccoli rabe, blanched in simmering water for 4 minutes and drained

10 whole cloves garlic, plus 2 cloves minced

1 cup fiddlehead ferns, blanched in simmering water for 4 minutes and drained

Zest and juice of 1 lemon

3 pounds Yukon gold potatoes, peeled and cut into 3-inch pieces

½ cup (1 stick) unsalted butter

½ cup low-sodium chicken broth

½ cup heavy cream

1. Season the salmon fillets with salt and pepper and rub with 2 tablespoons olive oil. Refrigerate until ready to cook.

2. In a large sauté pan, heat 2 tablespoons olive oil over medium heat. Add the broccoli rabe and minced garlic. Sauté over medium heat until the rabe is warm and the garlic is tender, about 6 minutes. Add the fiddlehead ferns and toss to combine. Continue to cook 1 minute more. Remove from the heat, add the lemon zest and juice, and season with salt and pepper. Toss to combine.

3. Place the potatoes in a medium saucepan, add 10 cloves garlic, and cover with water. Bring to a boil and simmer until the potatoes are tender, about 12 minutes. Drain the potatoes and garlic and return them to the pan.

4. Using a potato masher, mash the potatoes and garlic until broken up. Add the butter, broth, and heavy cream and mash vigorously until smooth. Taste and season with salt and pepper.

5. In a medium cast-iron skillet, heat the remaining ¼ cup olive oil over medium heat. Once the oil is shimmering and smoking a little, place the salmon in the pan, skin side down. Shallow fry to brown, 2 to 3 minutes. Flip and cook for 2 to 3 minutes more, until an instant-read thermometer inserted into the thickest part of a fillet is 122°F for wild, 124°F for farmed, or the fish is cooked to desired doneness. Rest the salmon on a plate, skin side up, for 5 minutes.

6. To serve, spoon mashed potato onto each of four plates and top each with a skin side up salmon fillet. Arrange broccoli rabe next to the fish. Sprinkle with a little more salt and a drizzle of olive oil.

POACHING

Poaching is a moist cooking method where you gently cook the fish in liquid at a temperature lower than a simmer. This is a gentle cooking method best suited to skinless, boneless fillet portions. When poaching, use a flavorful liquid—don't be shy with aromatics like shallots, garlic, fresh herbs, citrus, and spices. Be sure the poaching liquid will fully cover the salmon before cooking, then heat it before adding the fish. The liquid should be hot but not bubbling vigorously—aim for a temperature just below simmering, around 160 to 180°F. Once the liquid is at the proper temperature, slide the fish into the pan and let it cook gently to a medium doneness—10 to 12 minutes for a 1-inch-thick portion of salmon; less time if it is thinner. Poaching is the most delicate cooking method for fish. It's perfect for any type of lean, flaky fish that can easily overcook or fall apart with other methods.

HERE ARE SOME BASIC TIPS FOR POACHING:

SEASON THE FISH: At a minimum, use good-quality salt and pepper. If you have time, lightly cure the fish with salt (or a salt and sugar combination) and refrigerate for 30 minutes.

THE PAN: Be sure to use a pan large enough to fit all of the fish you will cook without overcrowding. I often use a 12-inch stainless steel pan with 4-inch sides that is large enough to fit 4 portions at once and deep enough that the poaching liquid covers the fish by ¾ to 1 inch.

THE LIQUID: You can use water, fish stock, wine, or a combination. Aromatics like onions, carrots, celery, herbs, and spices are often added to create a flavorful poaching liquid called court bouillon.

THE TEMPERATURE: Maintain a temperature just below simmering on an instant-read thermometer. You should see a few wisps of steam and tiny bubbles but no vigorous bubbling.

THE TECHNIQUE: Gently submerge the fish in the poaching liquid and cook until just opaque and flaky.

THE RIGHT TOOL: Transfer the fish to a plate using a fish spatula or a metal spatula large enough to lift the fish without it breaking.

OPPOSITE: The ferry terminal in Kingston, Washington, as seen from Puget Sound during king salmon season.

POACHED SALMON RILLETTES WITH BALSAMIC VINAIGRETTE SALAD

This recipe does require a bit of planning and some time, but it can be stored in the refrigerator for 3 to 5 days to make weeknight meal prep faster. The convenience more than offsets the time spent producing several jars of the rillette. You can use the rillette as a salad topper (as I do here) or in place of canned tuna in a sandwich or salad (it mixes well with fresh mayonnaise). Feel free to adjust with your favorite herbs and spices or a splash of chili garlic crunch for contrast.

SERVES 4

2 tablespoons kosher salt, plus more to taste

One 1½-pound skin-on, boneless salmon belly

½ cup peeled, diced cucumber

¼ cup diced, blanched carrot

¼ cup diced, blanched celery

2 teaspoons finely minced tarragon leaves

¼ cup plus 3 tablespoons extra-virgin olive oil

1 teaspoon sea salt, plus more to taste

1 teaspoon freshly ground black pepper, plus more to taste

2 tablespoons balsamic vinegar

1 teaspoon Dijon mustard

½ teaspoon garlic powder

3 to 4 leaves Tuscan kale

3 to 4 leaves romaine lettuce

3 to 4 leaves Bibb lettuce

½ cup shaved carrots

¼ cup dried strawberries

1. Preheat the oven to 200°F.

2. In a medium saucepan, bring 4 cups water and 2 tablespoons kosher salt to a simmer over medium-high heat. Add the salmon and poach for 8 minutes at about 185°F. Transfer the salmon to a cutting board and discard the water. Allow the salmon to cool for 5 to 6 minutes until safe to touch. Gently peel off the salmon skin. Pull the salmon meat apart into small flakes and place in a medium bowl.

3. Add the cucumber, carrot, celery, tarragon, 3 tablespoons olive oil, 1 teaspoon sea salt, and 1 teaspoon pepper to the bowl with the salmon and gently toss together. Taste and adjust salt and pepper.

4. Divide the salmon mixture equally into two 16-ounce glass mason jars, including the oil and liquid. Place the lids on the jars loosely and allow to cool to room temperature. Then tighten the lids and place in the refrigerator. Refrigerate for a minimum of 15 to 20 minutes.

5. When ready to serve, prepare the vinaigrette by whisking the balsamic vinegar and mustard in a small bowl. Whisk in the remaining ¼ cup olive oil and season with kosher salt, pepper, and garlic powder.

6. To make the salad, carefully tear the kale, romaine, and Bibb lettuces into bite-size pieces and place in a large bowl. Add the shaved carrots, dried strawberries, and vinaigrette and toss to combine. Season with kosher salt and pepper and toss to combine.

7. To serve, divide the dressed salad among each of four salad plates. Open one jar of salmon rillette, scoop out ¼ cup portions for each plate, and set on top of the salad.

OLIVE OIL–POACHED SALMON WITH SPICE TOPPING

As stated earlier, salmon is one of the most diverse proteins you can cook, and it responds well to being poached in olive oil. The result is a succulent and unctuous fillet with a texture like no other. Without a doubt, this is one of the most luxurious preparations you can make.

SERVES 4

SALMON

Four 4-ounce skinless, boneless salmon fillets

1 teaspoon kosher salt

¼ teaspoon freshly ground black pepper

½ cup extra-virgin olive oil, plus more for brushing

1 sprig fresh thyme

1 sprig fresh tarragon

¼ teaspoon fennel pollen

¼ teaspoon orange zest

¼ teaspoon pink peppercorn, toasted and roughly chopped

¼ teaspoon Maldon flaky sea salt

PETITE SALAD

¼ cup extra-virgin olive oil

2 tablespoons pea tendrils

4 to 5 chives, thinly sliced

1 radish, thinly sliced

½ teaspoons kosher salt

½ teaspoon freshly ground black pepper

1. **For the salmon,** season both sides of each fillet with the salt and pepper and place inside a zip-top bag with the olive oil, thyme, and tarragon; seal the bag.

2. In a medium pot, prepare a warm water bath that is sufficient to cover the bag of salmon. The water should register 140°F on an instant-read thermometer. Add the bag and cook until the internal temperature of the salmon reaches 105°F, about 20 minutes. This is super low for cooked salmon, but the result is very moist and tender. Just be extra careful when it comes to food safety. This includes handling the preparation and cooking with extra clean hands and a spotlessly clean work area. Low-temperature cooking requires good hygiene.

3. Remove the salmon from the bag to a serving plate. Brush the surface with olive oil and season with the fennel pollen, orange zest, pink peppercorn, and sea salt.

4. **For the petite salad,** combine the olive oil, pea tendrils, chives, radish, salt, and pepper in a small bowl and toss to combine.

5. Serve the salmon warm with the petite salad on the side.

POACHED SALMON WITH WINTER RADISH & BEETS

I discovered the wonderful flavor marriage between radishes and salmon while traveling in Kyoto, Japan. The plate used in this photo is from that trip. The bright flavor and crisp texture of the various radishes that I use elevate any salmon dish. Add the sweet flavor of the beets and the dish is complete.

SERVES 4

Four 3-ounce skinless, boneless salmon fillets

1 tablespoon kosher salt, plus more to taste

1 tablespoon granulated sugar

4 cups room-temperature water

1 lemon, sliced

1 bay leaf

1 teaspoon black peppercorns

2 red beets, trimmed, cooked, peeled, and quartered

2 golden beets, trimmed, cooked, peeled, and quartered

2 red winter radishes, trimmed and shaved paper-thin

¼ cup extra-virgin olive oil

2 tablespoons rice vinegar

1 tablespoon thinly sliced chives

Freshly ground black pepper

2 ounces arugula

2 ounces frisée

1. Place the salmon in a container that is large enough to fit the fillets. In a small bowl, combine the 1 tablespoon salt and sugar and dust over the salmon fillets. Cover loosely with plastic wrap and refrigerate for 1 hour.

2. Remove the fillets from the refrigerator. Rinse off the salt and sugar in ice-cold running water.

3. In a large saucepan, combine the 4 cups water, lemon slices, bay leaf, and peppercorns. Set over medium heat and bring to a simmer (about 185°F on an instant-read thermometer). Place the salmon fillets in the pan and gently poach for 10 minutes; do not let the liquid boil. Use a fish spatula to transfer the salmon to a plate and pat dry. Cover loosely with plastic wrap and refrigerate until chilled. Discard the poaching liquid.

4. In a medium bowl, combine the beets and radishes. Toss with the olive oil, vinegar, and chives, then season with salt and pepper. Add the arugula and frisée and toss gently to combine.

5. To serve, divide the beets and greens salad among each of four plates. Gently flake the poached salmon fillets into pieces and place on top of each salad. Drizzle with any vinaigrette remaining in the bowl.

POACHED

SALMON WITH GINGER, GARLIC & COCONUT BROTH

White miso is a fabulous flavor complement to salmon, adding deep umami and depth. For a simple meal, I sometimes mix a teaspoon of miso with two tablespoons mayonnaise and spread it over salmon before broiling. It's so easy, and it also pairs well with coconut and herbs. This recipe is flexible—you can use more or less miso to taste and increase or decrease the herbs and arugula. Steamed jasmine rice would also be a perfect accompaniment.

SERVES 4

One 1-pound skinless, boneless, salmon fillet, cut into 4 portions

½ teaspoon kosher salt, plus more to taste

½ teaspoon granulated sugar

¼ cup extra-virgin olive oil

1 large white onion, thinly sliced

5 cloves garlic, thinly sliced

2 tablespoons minced fresh ginger

¼ cup white miso paste

2 cups room-temperature water

¼ cup rice vinegar

One 13½-ounce can unsweetened organic full-fat coconut milk

2 ounces arugula

Freshly ground black pepper

2 limes, 1 juiced, 1 cut into 8 wedges

1 tablespoon chopped fresh basil

1 tablespoon chopped fresh mint

¼ cup toasted shredded coconut

1. Place the salmon in a shallow bowl. In a small bowl, combine ½ teaspoon salt and the sugar. Season the salmon fillet with the mixture, coating both sides. Cover loosely with plastic wrap and refrigerate for 30 minutes.

2. In a large, deep sauté pan, heat the olive oil over medium heat until shimmering. Add the onion and cover. Cook until softened and lightly caramelized, about 4 minutes, stirring occasionally as the onions steam and brown. Stir in the garlic and ginger and continue cooking, uncovered, until soft, 2 minutes.

3. Add the miso paste and stir until warmed and slightly browned, about 6 minutes. Stir in the water, vinegar, and coconut milk and bring to a gentle simmer. Add the chilled salmon pieces and continue simmering for 5 minutes. Add the arugula and cover again; no need to stir. Let the pan sit, covered, over the heat until the arugula is wilted and salmon is warmed through, 4 to 6 minutes. Uncover and taste the liquid. Add salt, pepper, and lime juice to taste.

4. To serve, place a fish fillet into each of four bowls and ladle some of the broth around the fish. Sprinkle with the basil and mint, and garnish with the toasted coconut and lime wedges, if desired.

FRENCH ROLLED OMELETTES WITH CREAMY POACHED SALMON & MOREL MUSHROOMS

A classic French omelette has a smooth, silky exterior with no browning and cradles a tender, moist, soft-scrambled interior. The technique for making one is something every cook should learn. Be sure to invest in a quality nonstick pan, as this is one of the keys to preparing a classic French omelette. Note that this is a lunch or dinner omelette, using three eggs per portion—so don't be alarmed. Morel mushrooms are typically found in the spring; feel free to substitute any mushroom that is available. Serve this dish on its own, with some of the creamy filling spooned over the top of the omelette, or accompanied by sautéed spinach, oven-roasted potatoes, or fresh fruit.

SERVES 4

SALMON

¾ cup room-temperature water

¼ cup dry white wine

1 sprig tarragon

1 sprig flat-leaf parsley

1 teaspoon kosher salt

½ teaspoon freshly ground black pepper

One 8-ounce skin-on, boneless, center-cut salmon fillet, cut in half

MORELS

2 tablespoons extra-virgin olive oil

2 tablespoons minced shallot

½ cup morel mushrooms, sliced or left whole if small

3 tablespoons dry sherry or Chardonnay

½ cup heavy cream

1 cup flaked salmon

1 tablespoon fresh fine herb mixture (equal parts chive, tarragon, chervil, and parsley)

Kosher salt and freshly ground white pepper

OMELETTES

12 large eggs

¼ cup half-and-half

1 teaspoon kosher salt

¼ teaspoon freshly ground white pepper

6 tablespoons unsalted butter, divided into 1½-tablespoon portions, plus more for brushing

1. **For the salmon,** bring the water, wine, tarragon, parsley, salt, and pepper to a simmer in a medium saucepan over medium heat. Once simmering, reduce the heat to medium-low. When the water is 180°F on an instant-read thermometer, add the salmon. Let cook gently for 6 minutes, then turn off the heat. Allow the salmon to cool in the liquid for 15 minutes. Once cool, transfer the salmon to a plate, pat dry, and peel off and discard the skin. Gently flake into a small bowl and reserve.

2. **For the morels,** heat the olive oil in a medium skillet over medium heat and gently sauté the shallots until softened, 3 to 4 minutes. Increase the heat to medium-high and add the morels, sautéing until they are tender and golden brown, 3 to 4 minutes.

3. Deglaze the pan with the sherry and reduce until little liquid remains, about 8 minutes. Add the heavy cream, salmon, and fine herb mixture and simmer on medium heat until the mixture is thick and creamy, 3 to 4 minutes. Season with salt and white pepper.

4. **For the omelettes,** whisk the eggs, half-and-half, salt, and pepper in a large bowl until completely blended, 1 to 2 minutes. Divide the egg mixture among four individual bowls or cups.

5. Heat 1½ tablespoons butter in a 9- or 10-inch nonstick skillet over medium-high heat. As soon as the butter melts and before it starts to sizzle, pour in one portion of the eggs. Stir in a circular pattern with a wooden spoon or rubber spatula to "scramble" the eggs while scraping down the sides of the pan. Continue stirring and shaking the pan until the eggs are soft but remain slightly liquid. (This is a fine line that requires practice and is the essence of a French rolled omelette.) As soon as the surface is wet but not runny, remove from the heat.

6. Starting at the handle side of the pan, use a rubber spatula to begin rolling the omelette into a cylinder shape; it takes about three rolls until the omelette is about 2 inches from the opposite side of the pan. Use the spatula to fold the last flap of egg over the top of the cylinder, leaving the seam side up.

7. Slide the omelette to the edge of the pan. Flip it onto a plate with the seam side down. Even out the shape, if necessary. You can tuck in the ends if you like. Brush the surface with a bit of butter.

8. To serve, spoon equal portions of the creamy salmon-mushroom mixture onto the top of each omelette. Serve at once.

POACHED SALMON WITH TUSCAN KALE, GRAPES & LEMON

I prefer to poach salmon with the skin on and then peel it off afterward. People often ask why. The reason is moisture retention. From my experience, poaching with the skin on yields a more succulent end result compared to poached skin-off salmon. The contrasting sweet flavor of the grapes, bitter of the kale, and citrus sour of the lemon work well together and add punch to the recipe. Optional garnishes can include baby greens, herb flowers, and blanched multicolor cauliflower florets.

SERVES 4 ✳ COOK TO 122°F FOR WILD, 124°F FOR FARMED, OR TO DESIRED DONENESS

2 cups dry white wine

1 lemon, zested, juiced, and quartered

⅓ cup kosher salt, plus more to taste

8 black peppercorns

Four 4-ounce skin-on, boneless, center-cut salmon fillets

¼ cup extra-virgin olive oil

1 bunch Tuscan kale, sliced into ribbons

Freshly ground black pepper

1 clove garlic, minced

½ cup halved red grapes

1 cup heavy cream

Fresh herbs or thinly sliced chives for garnish

1. Combine 8 cups cold water with the wine, lemon quarters (reserve the lemon and juice for Step 3), ⅓ cup salt, and peppercorns in a large pot. Bring to a simmer over medium heat, then reduce the heat to low to bring the water to a temperature of 180°F on an instant-read thermometer. Add the salmon fillets and poach about 10 minutes, until the instant-read thermometer inserted in the thickest part of a fillet is 122°F for wild, 124°F for farmed, or the fish is cooked to desired doneness. Use a fish spatula to transfer the fillets to a plate. Discard the poaching liquid. Let the fillets rest for 4 to 5 minutes. When cool enough to handle, peel off and discard the skin.

2. Heat the olive oil in a medium sauté pan over medium heat. Add the kale, season with salt and pepper, and stir. Reduce the heat to low, add the garlic, and stir, then cover with a lid. Allow the kale to gently wilt, about 8 minutes. Once wilted, add the grapes, then remove from the heat.

3. Place the heavy cream in a small saucepan and reduce over medium heat by one-third. Once reduced, add the lemon zest and juice, and season with salt and pepper. Stir while gently warming. Reserve.

4. To serve, divide the sautéed kale and grapes among four plates. For each serving, spoon 2 tablespoons of the lemon cream onto a plate and top with a portion of salmon. Garnish with fresh herbs or thinly sliced chives.

POACHED FLAKED SALMON WITH CUCUMBER, CORIANDER & CHERRY TOMATOES

Some of the recipes I share are derived from my time working as a chef in a commercial kitchen; others are examples of quick-to-prepare items I have made at home. This one requires easy-to-find ingredients, isn't costly, and is quick to prepare—the perfect weeknight dinner solution. You can also prepare the salad mixture and salmon components one day ahead and combine them the day of for a quick take-to-work lunch option. The poached salmon remains succulent even after refrigeration.

SERVES 4 ✳ COOK TO 122°F FOR WILD, 124°F FOR FARMED, OR TO DESIRED DONENESS

Kosher salt

½ cup extra-virgin olive oil

⅓ cup rice vinegar

Four 4-ounce skinless, boneless salmon fillets

1 medium head romaine lettuce, chopped

½ pint cherry tomatoes, halved

1 English cucumber, peeled and diced

¼ bunch flat-leaf parsley, roughly chopped

1 teaspoon ground coriander

1 teaspoon freshly ground black pepper

1. In a medium saucepan over medium-high heat, bring 4 cups cold water, a pinch of salt, 2 tablespoons of the olive oil, and 2 tablespoons of the vinegar to a simmer. Reduce the heat so the poaching liquid is just simmering and add the salmon fillets. Simmer 8 to 10 minutes, until an instant-read thermometer inserted in the thickest part of a fillet is 122°F for wild, 124°F for farmed, or the fish is cooked to desired doneness.

2. Use a fish spatula to transfer the salmon to a plate; discard the liquid. Allow the salmon to cool at room temperature for 15 minutes, then transfer the plate to the refrigerator to chill for 30 minutes.

3. In a large bowl, toss together the lettuce, tomatoes, cucumber, parsley, coriander, pepper, and the remaining olive oil and vinegar until fully coated. Taste and season with salt, if needed.

4. Divide the salad among four salad plates. Flake each fillet into large pieces and place on top of a salad.

POACHED

SALMON GINGER NORI RICE BOWL

This dish can be made in advance and served warm or chilled. If you make a large batch, refrigerate portions for up to 3 days, making it a grab-and-go lunch option. To elevate it further, mix two tablespoons of mayonnaise with one teaspoon white miso paste and drizzle over the top. I use sharp kitchen shears to cut the nori sheets, so they are nice and fine.

SERVES 4

- One 1-pound skinless, boneless salmon fillet, cut into ½-inch chunks
- 1 teaspoon kosher salt, plus more to taste
- 1 cup thinly sliced Swiss chard
- One ½-inch piece fresh ginger, peeled and shaved paper-thin
- 2 scallions, thinly sliced
- ½ cup shredded carrots
- Freshly ground black pepper
- 2 cups Cooked Sushi Rice (recipe follows)
- 1 sheet nori, cut into 12 pieces
- ½ teaspoon toasted sesame oil
- ½ teaspoon sesame seeds

1. Put the salmon in a bowl, sprinkle with the salt, and toss to coat. Let rest for 10 minutes.

2. Place the chard, ginger, and ½ cup water in a medium saucepan over medium heat. Cook, covered, until the chard is just tender, 4 to 5 minutes. Top the chard with the salmon and cover. Cook for 5 minutes, then remove from the heat and allow to sit, covered, for 3 minutes more. Uncover, add the scallions and carrots, and toss. The heat from the salmon mixture will slightly wilt the carrots and scallion. Season with salt and pepper.

3. Divide the rice among four medium bowls. Top with the salmon mixture. Garnish each bowl with nori pieces, a drizzle of sesame oil, and some of the sesame seeds.

COOKED SUSHI RICE

MAKES ABOUT 3 CUPS

- 1½ cups sushi rice (see Note)
- 2 cups room-temperature water
- 1 teaspoon kosher salt
- 2 tablespoons rice vinegar
- 2 teaspoons granulated sugar
- ¼ teaspoon dried ginger powder

1. Place the rice in a fine-mesh sieve and rinse under cold running water until the water runs clear, 3 to 4 minutes. Shake to remove excess water and place the rice in a rice cooker or small saucepan. Add the water and salt. Start the rice cooker or bring the water to a boil over medium heat. Once boiling, reduce the heat to low, cover, and cook until the water is fully absorbed, 16 to 18 minutes. Remove from the heat.

2. In a small bowl, combine the vinegar, sugar, and ginger powder. Scoop the warm rice into a medium bowl and add the vinegar-sugar mixture. Gently toss to combine, then cool to room temperature, about 20 minutes. The rice is now ready to use. Leftover rice can be refrigerated in an airtight container for up to 5 days.

Note: I use organic sushi rice from California, which you can find at supermarkets or online.

POACHED SALMON WITH SWEET PEAS & RADISH

This recipe is best in late spring when peas are fresh and sweet and local radishes are starting to become available. Though optional, serving with Osetra caviar is a wonderful enhancement. You can find excellent-quality caviar at higher-end supermarkets across the US or through my preferred online source, Citarella of New York City.

SERVES 4 ✳ COOK TO 122°F FOR WILD, 124°F FOR FARMED, OR TO DESIRED DONENESS

2 cups dry white wine

Finely grated zest and juice of 1 lemon, spent lemon quartered

⅓ cup kosher salt, plus more to taste

8 black peppercorns

Four 4-ounce skinless, boneless salmon loin fillets

¼ cup extra-virgin olive oil

1 cup sweet peas, preferably freshly shucked

12 French breakfast or red radishes, quartered

Freshly ground black pepper

1 teaspoon thinly sliced chives

2 teaspoons farmed Osetra caviar (optional)

1. Combine 8 cups cold water, the wine, lemon juice and quarters, ⅓ cup salt, and the peppercorns in a large pot. Bring to a simmer over medium-high heat. Reduce the heat to low and bring the water to 160°F on an instant-read thermometer. Add the salmon and poach about 10 minutes, until the instant-read thermometer inserted in the thickest part of a fillet is 122°F for wild, 124°F for farmed, or the fish is cooked to desired doneness. Use a fish spatula to transfer the salmon to a plate. Reserve ⅓ cup of the poaching liquid and discard the rest.

2. While the salmon poaches, heat the olive oil in a medium sauté pan over medium heat. Add the peas and radishes and stir. Season with salt and pepper. Reduce the heat to low, cover, and cook for 5 minutes.

3. Off the heat, add the lemon zest, chives, and reserved poaching liquid. Stir and season with salt and pepper.

4. To serve, spoon the sautéed peas and radishes along with 1 tablespoon of the sauce on each of four plates. Set a fillet on each plate. Spoon ½ teaspoon of the caviar on top of each salmon fillet, if using. Serve at once.

POACHED SALMON WITH CHARRED CAESAR SALAD

I love serving poached salmon with Caesar dressing—it's delicious. If you have a rind of Parmigiano-Reggiano in your fridge, you can use it to add umami to the poaching liquid. You can poach the salmon a day ahead and store it in the refrigerator to make this a quick and easy weeknight dish.

SERVES 4 * COOK TO 122°F FOR WILD, 124°F FOR FARMED, OR TO DESIRED DONENESS

CAESAR SALAD

1 head romaine lettuce, outer leaves and heart separated

⅔ cup mayonnaise

2 teaspoons Dijon mustard

2 teaspoons freshly squeezed lemon juice

4 oil-packed anchovy fillets

1 clove garlic

½ teaspoon freshly ground black pepper, plus more for finishing

⅓ cup Parmesan cheese, grated, plus more for finishing

Kosher salt

2 teaspoons extra-virgin olive oil

SALMON

⅓ cup kosher salt

2 tablespoons granulated sugar

8 black peppercorns

Zest of 1 lemon

Small Parmigiano-Reggiano rind (optional)

Four 4-ounce skinless, boneless center-cut salmon fillets

½ cup toasted croutons for serving

1 tablespoon Maldon flaky sea salt

1. **For the Caesar salad,** place the outer lettuce leaves in a blender with the mayonnaise, mustard, lemon juice, anchovies, garlic, black pepper, and Parmesan. Start blending on medium speed and gradually increase to high speed. Blend until smooth. The texture should coat the back of a spoon. Taste and adjust for salt and pepper. Transfer to an airtight container and refrigerate until ready to use.

2. Preheat the broiler to high. Split the romaine heart into quarters lengthwise. Place on a baking sheet, drizzle lightly with the olive oil, and transfer to the broiler. Broil until lightly charred and golden brown around the edges but not burnt, 5 to 7 minutes.

3. **For the salmon,** in a medium saucepan combine 8 cups cold water with the salt, sugar, peppercorns, lemon zest, and cheese rind, if using. Heat over medium until the liquid reaches 155°F on an instant-read thermometer. Maintain this temperature.

4. Add the salmon to the poaching liquid and be sure it is submerged (add more water, if needed). Cook about 10 minutes, until the instant-read thermometer inserted in the thickest part of a fillet is 122°F for wild, 124°F for farmed, or the fish is cooked to desired doneness. The salmon will be tender and flaky. Use a fish spatula to transfer the salmon to a plate and set aside. Discard the poaching liquid.

5. To serve, add a good dollop of chilled Caesar dressing to each of four plates. Place a lettuce quarter on each plate and sprinkle with pepper and Parmesan. Top each with salmon pieces and a few croutons and season with a drizzle of olive oil and a pinch of sea salt. Optional: Garnish with thin radish slices.

清助

RAW

Raw salmon dishes like sushi and sashimi have gained immense popularity globally. Their appealing texture, rich flavor, and vibrant color make them a favorite choice for raw consumption. Beyond traditional Japanese fare, raw salmon is increasingly incorporated into other preparations such as carpaccio, crudo, and tartare.

However, the consumption of raw salmon must be done carefully and with food safety in mind. A key food safety measure to mitigate risk is freezing the salmon to a specific temperature for a specific amount of time. The FDA recommends freezing fish intended for raw consumption at an ambient temperature of -31°F or below until solid and storing at an ambient temperature of -4°F or below for 24 hours prior to thawing and consuming. This deep-freezing process effectively kills any potential parasites present in the fish, rendering it safe for raw consumption. Note that freezing at -31°F or below requires specialized equipment and is not something a domestic freezer can do.

Consuming raw salmon that has not been properly frozen so that it is "sashimi grade" carries risks. Therefore, it is paramount to purchase raw salmon from reputable sources that can guarantee the fish has undergone the necessary freezing process to ensure its safety. Asking your retailer about their sourcing and handling practices is a crucial step to protect your health when eating raw salmon. Do not prepare and consume raw salmon if you are unsure of how to properly manage and maintain food safety.

HERE ARE SOME BASIC TIPS FOR HANDLING AND SERVING RAW FISH:

PRACTICE IMPECCABLE HYGIENE: Wash your hands thoroughly with soap and hot water for at least 30 seconds before and after handling raw salmon. Make sure all knives, tools, and serving plates are thoroughly clean and sanitized.

ENSURE SALMON WAS PROPERLY FROZEN: For raw consumption, salmon must be frozen to -4°F or colder for at least 7 days to effectively kill potential pathogens.

THAW SAFELY: If frozen, thaw salmon slowly in the refrigerator overnight, never at room temperature.

SOURCE "SUSHI-GRADE" SALMON: Purchase salmon specifically labeled "sushi-grade" or "sashimi-grade" from a reputable supplier to ensure it has been handled and processed correctly.

MAINTAIN STRICT COLD CHAIN: Keep raw salmon refrigerated between 32°F and 34°F at all times—from purchase until immediate preparation and serving.

PREVENT CROSS-CONTAMINATION: Use a separate cutting board and razor-sharp clean knife when cutting raw salmon.

CONSUME PROPERLY: Serve and consume raw salmon immediately after preparation.

OPPOSITE: Traditional fishing boats and a blue salmon-farm tender in the harbor near Punta Blanca in Calbuco, Chile.

SALMON CHIRASHI WITH ORANGE & PICKLED GINGER DRESSING & SANSHO PEPPER

Chirashi, meaning "scattered" in Japanese, is a vibrant and colorful dish consisting of vinegared sushi rice topped with a variety of fresh ingredients. I tasted multiple versions using salmon during trips to Toyosu Market and Tsukiji Outer Market in Tokyo. This version features delicate slices of raw salmon lightly cured with ginger, served with a tangy orange and pickled ginger dressing.

SERVES 4

SALMON

One 1-pound sashimi-grade skinless, boneless center-cut salmon fillet

½ teaspoon kosher salt

½ teaspoon granulated sugar

½ teaspoon powdered ginger

SUSHI RICE

¼ cup rice vinegar

¼ cup distilled white vinegar

¼ cup granulated sugar

1 teaspoon kosher salt

1½ cups sushi rice

DRESSING

¼ cup seasoned rice vinegar

¼ cup mirin

2 tablespoons tamari

½ teaspoon instant dashi granules

2 ounces pickled ginger with juice

3 scallions, washed and thinly sliced

Zest and juice of 3 Cara Cara oranges (see Notes)

Salt and freshly ground black pepper

---

1 cup blanched, shelled edamame

1 ripe avocado, pitted, peeled, and thinly sliced

½ cup pickled radish

1 tablespoon pickled ginger, finely chopped

1 sheet nori seaweed, toasted and cut into thin strips

Sesame seeds

Sansho pepper powder (see Notes)

1. **For the salmon,** place the fillet on a plate and season all over with the salt, sugar, and powdered ginger. Cover loosely with plastic wrap and refrigerate for 30 minutes.

2. **For the sushi rice,** combine 1½ cups cold water, the vinegars, sugar, and salt in a medium saucepan. Lightly rinse the rice, add to the pan, and stir well. Bring to a boil over high heat, then cover and reduce the heat to low. Cook until the liquid is absorbed and the rice is tender, about 10 minutes.

3. **For the dressing,** whisk the vinegar, mirin, tamari, dashi, pickled ginger, and scallions in a medium bowl. Allow the dressing to rest for 15 minutes so the flavors meld. Add the zest to the dressing. Halve one of the oranges and juice it into the dressing. Carefully cut segments from the remaining 2 oranges. Add the orange segments to the dressing and stir. Season with salt and pepper.

4. To assemble the chirashi bowls, cut the salmon into large cubes. Divide the rice among four bowls and garnish with the edamame, avocado, and pickled radish and ginger. Top each bowl with some cubes of salmon and drizzle with the dressing. Finish with nori strips, sesame seeds, and a sprinkle of sansho pepper powder.

Notes:

Cara Cara oranges are a crossbreed of Washington navel and the Brazilian Bahia orange. They are juicy and sweet and can be found in the US from December to April.

Sansho pepper comes from the peppercorn of the Japanese pepper plant (*Zanthoxylum piperitum*), also known as the Japanese prickly-ash. Known for its tongue-tingling effect and notes of citrus, it pairs well with orange and ginger. You can buy dried green sansho peppercorns whole or as a powder online. It is a common table condiment in Japan.

SALMON POKE WITH CUCUMBER & HERBS

This recipe calls for salmon trim and belly meat. When trimming and portioning a salmon fillet, there are bits and pieces of trim that are delicious and perfectly good to eat but too odd in shape or too small for a proper center-of-the-plate portion. This recipe utilizes those off cuts. I usually accumulate and freeze salmon trim in a zip-top plastic bag and then thaw and utilize it for various recipes, including this poke. Note that I also use maple sugar, which is reduced and crystallized maple syrup. You can find it online.

SERVES 4

1 tablespoon maple sugar

1 tablespoon kosher salt, plus more to taste

2 teaspoons ginger powder

12 ounces skinless, boneless salmon trim and belly, cut into ½-inch cubes

1 English cucumber, peeled and cut into ½-inch cubes

1 shallot, halved and sliced paper-thin

1 medium carrot, peeled and julienned

1 rib celery, finely diced

1 cup julienned red cabbage

¼ cup rice vinegar

¼ cup extra-virgin olive oil

Freshly ground black pepper

2 cups cooked Sushi Rice (see recipe, page 186)

¼ bunch fresh dill, sprigs picked

2 teaspoons Merkén or chipotle chili powder

1. In a small bowl, combine the maple sugar, salt, and ginger powder. Place the salmon cubes in a medium bowl and sprinkle the mixture over the cubes, stirring to evenly coat them. Cover loosely with plastic wrap and refrigerate for 1 hour.

2. In a large bowl, toss together the cucumber, shallot, carrot, celery, cabbage, vinegar, and olive oil. Season with salt and pepper. Cover loosely with plastic wrap and refrigerate for 1 hour.

3. When ready to serve, transfer the chilled salmon to the cucumber mixture and gently toss to combine. Taste and adjust with salt and pepper.

4. Divide the sushi rice among four bowls, then top with the poke and garnish with dill and a dusting of Merkén.

SALMON TATAKI WITH PICKLED VEGETABLES

Tataki is a Japanese cooking technique in which the fish or meat is seared very briefly over a high heat, then marinated in a flavorful sauce. It is a delicate and refreshing dish that highlights the clean flavors of the sashimi-grade salmon. You can use many types of vegetables to make pickles. You can also use various cuts, from a large dice to a julienne. Choose your favorite vegetable and use the mason jar method, below, to make a test batch.

SERVES 4

10 red radishes, diced

One 2-inch piece medium daikon radish, peeled and cut into medium dice

1 small carrot, peeled and cut into ¼-inch dice

½ cup rice vinegar

1 scallion, thinly sliced

1 clove garlic, minced

1 tablespoon minced fresh ginger

1 tablespoon plus ½ teaspoon kosher salt

1 tablespoon plus ½ teaspoon granulated sugar

One 1-pound sashimi-grade skinless, boneless center-cut salmon loin, fat line removed

½ teaspoon powdered ginger

Extra-virgin olive oil for coating

High-quality aged soy sauce for serving (optional)

1. Place the red and daikon radishes and carrots into individual 4-ounce mason jars (don't combine them). In a measuring cup, combine the vinegar, scallion, garlic, fresh ginger, 1 tablespoon salt, and 1 tablespoon sugar. Stir until fully combined. (You will have about ¾ cup pickling liquid.) Pour one-third of the pickling liquid over each of the three vegetables. Stir to coat the contents with the pickling liquid. Refrigerate, covered, for at least 24 hours to gently pickle.

2. Place the salmon on a plate and season with ½ teaspoon salt, ½ teaspoon sugar, and the powdered ginger. Cover loosely with plastic wrap and refrigerate for 30 minutes.

3. Place the chilled salmon on a small stainless-steel baking sheet coated with olive oil. Preheat the broiler on high or use a blow torch and lightly brown the top side of the salmon until golden, 60 to 90 seconds. Let cool, then cut the loin into 8 to 12 equal slices.

4. For each serving, spoon 2 tablespoons of the diced pickled vegetables onto a small plate. Top with 3 slices of the salmon. Drizzle with pickling liquid. Optional: Garnish each serving with a *kinome* leaf sprig. Serve with soy sauce on the side, if using. You can also serve a plate of lightly pickled grated carrots, red onion and shallot slices, and shaved radish on the side.

SALMON SUSHI & FRESH PICKLED GINGER

Sushi preparation is an art form that requires mastery to achieve excellent results. However, it is possible to produce fairly good sushi at home that competes with the product sold at supermarkets. This recipe serves as a guide. If you cook rice on a regular basis, it is worthwhile to buy a good-quality rice cooker. Stovetop rice is good, but the result is not as consistent as that of a rice cooker, particularly when making sushi rice. Also note that fresh pickled ginger is super easy to make and something I keep in my refrigerator. Sushi and sashimi are wildly popular, so give them a try.

SERVES 4

One 1-pound skinless, boneless sashimi-grade salmon belly

2 tablespoons rice vinegar

SUSHI RICE

2 cups short grain Japanese sushi rice

2 tablespoons granulated sugar

2 teaspoons kosher salt

½ cup rice vinegar

PICKLED GINGER

¼ cup rice vinegar

¼ cup distilled white vinegar

¼ cup granulated sugar

2 tablespoons kosher salt

One 1-inch knob ginger

Prepared wasabi for serving

1. Trim the salmon belly into a rectangle that is roughly 1 inch thick by 2 inches wide by 5 inches long. Wrap tightly in plastic and place in the freezer for 1 hour to firm up (not until it's solid). Partial freezing makes the fish easier to slice.

2. Combine 2½ cups water and the rice vinegar in a medium bowl and refrigerate until ready to make the rice balls.

3. **For the sushi rice,** place the rice in a fine-mesh sieve and rinse under cold running water until the water runs clear, 2 to 3 minutes. Shake the sieve to remove excess water and transfer the rice to a medium saucepan or rice cooker with 3 cups cold water. Start the rice cooker or bring the water to a boil over medium-high heat, then cover, reduce the heat to low, and cook until the water is fully absorbed and the rice is tender, 10 minutes. Remove from the heat and keep covered for 4 to 5 minutes. Transfer the rice to a large bowl.

4. In a small saucepan over low heat, dissolve the sugar and salt in the rice vinegar. Let the vinegar liquid cool to room temperature. Pour over the rice and gently fold with a wooden spoon to combine. Let cool for 15 to 20 minutes to allow the vinegar to absorb and to make it easier to handle.

5. **For the pickled ginger,** combine the vinegars, sugar, and salt in a small saucepan and bring to a simmer over medium-high heat. Using a mandoline, carefully cut thin slices of ginger lengthwise—as thin as you can safely shave them (always use the protective hand guard). Add the shaved ginger to the simmering vinegar and immediately remove from the heat. Cool at room temperature, 20 to 25 minutes. Place the ginger in an airtight container and refrigerate until ready to use. It will last up to 1 week.

6. You will need a well-sharpened knife to slice the salmon. Position the salmon belly flat on the cutting board and slice against the grain, using a gentle, smooth motion. Aim for slices of uniform ¼- to ½-inch thickness to achieve the ideal texture and presentation. Lay each salmon slice on a flat plate lined with plastic wrap. Once sliced, refrigerate.

7. To make the sushi, lightly dampen your hands with the chilled water–rice vinegar mixture to prevent the rice from sticking. Scoop out a walnut-size portion of the cooled sushi rice and place it

in the palm of your hand. Gently form the rice into an oblong or oval ball, using soft, pressing motions. The shape doesn't have to be perfect. Press to assure the rice sticks together and holds its shape. Dab a pea-size dot of wasabi in the center of the oval and lay a slice of salmon over the top. Press the fish gently to adhere and place the sushi on a plate. Keep working until you have 18 to 20 pieces of sushi.

8. Serve the sushi on a platter garnished with the pickled ginger and additional wasabi.

SALMON POKE WITH PONZU SAUCE

Ponzu sauce is simple to make, but the ingredients matter: Buy good-quality bonito flakes and mirin. Eden brand bonito is quite good for the price, but my preferred online source is Dashi Okume (you can buy the hijiki there as well). Combine the ingredients and let them meld overnight in the refrigerator at a minimum but longer if possible. I usually make three times the amount of this recipe and refrigerate it for a full week. The flavor development is remarkable and, once strained, it lasts for another week. Use it as a marinade, as done in this recipe, or brush it over salmon fillets just before broiling as a flavor amplifier.

SERVES 4

¾ cup gluten-free tamari

1 cup bonito flakes

¾ cup mirin

Zest and juice of 2 limes

1 tablespoon sesame oil

¼ cup dried hijiki

One 1-pound skinless, boneless sashimi-grade salmon belly, cut into ½-inch cubes

Cooked rice, avocado, spicy mayonnaise, sliced green onions (green parts only), and diced cucumber for serving

1. In a medium bowl, combine the tamari, bonito flakes, mirin, and lime zest and juice. Cover loosely with plastic wrap and refrigerate. Let steep for at least 24 hours and up to 3 days. To use, strain the desired amount through a fine-mesh sieve into a small bowl and blend with the sesame oil.

2. In a medium bowl, soak the hijiki in 1 cup warm water for 30 minutes. Strain.

3. In a large bowl, combine the salmon cubes with the ponzu sauce and hijiki and stir. Cover loosely with plastic wrap and refrigerate for 20 minutes.

4. Scoop cooked rice into each of four bowls. Divide the salmon among the bowls and top with avocado, spicy mayonnaise, green onion, and cucumber.

SALMON KOHLRABI-APPLE CRUDO WITH GOCHUJANG DRESSING

Autumn in New England brings delicious heirloom apples and sweet, tender kohlrabi—a brassica vegetable that gets no respect. I love combining kohlrabi with apples every time the weather starts to turn. Years ago, one of my students from Korea first introduced me to *ganjang* (Korean soy sauce), gochujang, and gochugaru pepper. His family owns an artisan fermentary that makes ganjang using a 600-year-old recipe, and his mom, Jonghee Kim, sent me samples of her soy sauce. I've been using it ever since. You can find her Artisan Fermentary soy sauce online at Gotham Grove and Regalis.

SERVES 4

One 1-pound sashimi-grade skinless, boneless salmon fillet, cut into 1-inch cubes

½ teaspoon kosher salt, plus more to taste

½ teaspoon light brown sugar

¼ cup rice vinegar

¼ cup extra-virgin olive oil

2 tablespoons ganjang (see Notes)

2 tablespoons gochujang paste (see Notes)

1 tablespoon minced fresh ginger

¼ cup dried golden raisins

2 tablespoons thinly sliced scallion

Freshly ground black pepper

1 ripe medium kohlrabi, peeled and thinly sliced on a mandoline

1 large Honeycrisp apple, peeled, halved, cored, thinly sliced, and soaked in lemon water

Gochugaru pepper flakes for garnish (optional)

Honey powder for garnish (optional)

1. Place the salmon cubes in a bowl and toss with ½ teaspoon salt and the brown sugar. Toss until fully coated. Cover loosely with plastic wrap and refrigerate until ready to use.

2. In a small bowl, whisk the vinegar, olive oil, ganjang, gochujang, ginger, raisins, and scallions. Taste the dressing and adjust with salt and pepper.

3. Place the kohlrabi slices in a large bowl. Drain the apples, pat dry, and add them to the bowl. Add the cubed salmon to the kohlrabi and apple slices, then drizzle with the dressing and toss together. Cover loosely with plastic wrap and allow to marinate in the refrigerator for 10 to 15 minutes. Serve cold. As an optional garnish, sprinkle gochugaru pepper flakes and a light dusting of honey powder over the crudo before serving.

Notes:

Gochugaru pepper is made in Korea from dried capsicum annuum.

A ***jang*** is a food made by fermenting soybeans. The three most common types of jang are *ganjang* (soy sauce), *doenjang* (soybean paste), and *gochujang* (chile paste). Jangs are used in place of salt to season foods and add a boost of umami deliciousness. They are wonderful to pair with any type of seafood.

SMOKED SALMON WINTER ENDIVE SALAD

Smoked salmon is extremely popular and the number one seafood sold at breakfast in the United States. However, I love to serve it for lunch and dinner, too. This luncheon salad is best when made at the last minute to maintain the texture of the frisée and the delicate flavor of the smoked salmon. Note the use of radicchio di castelfranco. I use it for the speckled color and texture, which add a nice contrast to the dish. If you aren't a fan of bitter lettuces like radicchio and endive, replace them with baby gem lettuces or your baby greens of choice. Serve slices of toasted ciabatta bread on the side. If served at breakfast, top with a poached egg.

SERVES 4

¼ cup extra-virgin olive oil

1 tablespoon white wine vinegar

1 teaspoon freshly squeezed lemon juice

½ teaspoon whole-grain mustard

½ teaspoon honey

1 tablespoon finely chopped fresh dill, plus sprigs for garnish

½ teaspoon kosher salt

½ teaspoon freshly ground black pepper

1 small head frisée, leaves separated

1 head radicchio di castelfranco, leaves separated

1 head red endive, leaves separated

8 ounces high-quality smoked salmon, thinly sliced

1. In a small bowl, whisk the olive oil, vinegar, lemon juice, mustard, honey, and chopped dill until incorporated. Season with the salt and pepper and set aside.

2. In a large bowl, gently toss the frisée, radicchio, and endive with about half of the dill vinaigrette. The lettuces should be lightly coated.

3. Place the dressed salad in the center of each of four plates or bowls. Arrange two or three slices of the smoked salmon on the salad. Drizzle the remaining vinaigrette over the smoked salmon. Garnish with a few dill sprigs. Serve chilled.

SALMON TARTARE SALAD WITH CUCUMBERS & BABY GREENS

This recipe is a composed salad where the salmon serves as the base. When combined with the vegetable garnish and mayonnaise, the end result can be used as a salad topper or a sandwich filler. I love using it for both. Once prepared, the composed salad can be kept in the refrigerator in an airtight container for up to 3 days. Since this is served raw, I suggest buying sashimi-grade salmon from a reputable vendor. Sashimi salmon is frozen at -60°F for at least 24 hours. Red's Best out of Boston does a wonderful job producing sashimi-grade seafood, and sells their product online.

SERVES 4

One 12-ounce skinless, boneless sashimi-grade salmon belly

1 teaspoon kosher salt, plus more to taste

1 teaspoon organic raw sugar

¼ cup sliced red onion

2 tablespoons jarred pickle juice

¼ cup diced English cucumbers

¼ cup diced kosher dill pickles

1 tablespoon thinly sliced chives

½ cup mayonnaise

1 teaspoon prepared wasabi

Freshly ground black pepper

Baby greens and fresh herbs for garnish

4 slices sourdough bread, toasted, for serving

1. Season the salmon with 1 teaspoon kosher salt and the sugar. Place in a glass baking dish and cover with plastic wrap. Refrigerate for 1 hour to cure.

2. Meanwhile, place the onion slices in a small bowl with the pickle juice.

3. Once the salmon has cured, dice into ½-inch pieces. Place in a medium bowl with the pickled red onion, cucumbers, pickles, chives, mayonnaise, and wasabi paste. Stir gently to combine. Taste and season with salt and pepper as needed.

4. To serve, spoon 2 to 3 tablespoons of the salmon mixture onto each of four plates. Top with the baby greens and herbs and serve with toasted sourdough on the side.

ROASTING

Roasting is a cooking method that uses dry heat to cook food evenly on all sides within an oven or enclosed space. It's one of the oldest and most versatile cooking techniques, and it is used for everything from whole salmon to smaller individual portions. Roasting relies on hot air to cook food. This dry heat creates a beautifully browned exterior and a tender, juicy interior. Roasting typically happens at temperatures of 300°F or higher. This high heat helps to caramelize the surface of the food and develop complex flavors. I roast salmon at 400°F for the first 3 to 4 minutes to accelerate browning and then reduce the temperature to 325°F to finish. In most cases, I actually use my high-end toaster oven for roasting rather than heat a larger oven. If you have a convection function on your oven, use it for the first few minutes. Convection causes the hot air to circulate around the food, cooking it evenly on all sides.

HERE ARE SOME BASIC TIPS FOR ROASTING:

DRY THE FISH: Pat the salmon dry with paper towels before seasoning and cooking to increase the potential for browning.

SEASON THE FISH: At a minimum, use good-quality salt and pepper. If you have time, lightly cure the fish with salt (or a salt and sugar combination) and refrigerate for at least 30 minutes.

RUB WITH OIL: Lightly coat the fish with oil. I use good-quality olive oil.

USE THE RIGHT PAN: Use a heavy-duty baking sheet lined with oil-rubbed foil.

USE A WIRE RACK: I use small stainless-steel racks and place the fish on them before roasting. This increases air circulation and helps brown both top and bottom.

USE THE BEST HEAT: Start hot at 400°F, then reduce to 325°F to finish.

DON'T OVERCOOK: Salmon cooks quickly, so keep an eye on it. Insert an instant-read digital thermometer in the thickest part of the fillet and take a reading to determine if the fish is cooked (122°F for wild, 124°F for farmed, or to preference). The thickest part of the salmon will be opaque and flake easily with a fork.

LET THE FISH REST: Once the desired temperature is reached, remove the salmon from the oven and let it rest for a few minutes on a plate, skin side up if there is skin.

USE THE RIGHT TOOL: Transfer the fish to a plate using a roasting fork, fish spatula, or a metal spatula large enough to lift the fish without it breaking.

OPPOSITE: Traditional stilt homes, or *palafitos*, near the town of Castro on Chiloé Island, Chile. Chiloé is a historic center for salmon farming in Chilean Patagonia.

ROASTED SALMON WITH GINGER-GARLIC CHILI CRISP

Chili crisp has become a popular salmon topping and is easy to prepare. Serve it over a roasted fillet or salmon steak. The high-heat cooking causes the fish to caramelize, which complements the flavor of the crisp. I add pickled ginger for sweetness. If you purchase premade chili crisp for convenience, you can still blend in the pickled ginger for flavor. Curing the salmon in a ginger, maple, and kosher salt dusting brings all the ingredients together.

SERVES 4 ✳ COOK TO 122°F FOR WILD, 124°F FOR FARMED, OR TO DESIRED DONENESS

1 teaspoon kosher salt

½ teaspoon maple sugar

1 teaspoon ginger powder, plus more for finishing

Four 4-ounce skin-on, boneless center-cut salmon fillets

1 tablespoon extra-virgin olive oil

Ginger-Garlic Chili Crisp (recipe follows)

1. In a small bowl, combine the salt, maple sugar, and ginger powder and season the salmon fillets all over with the mixture. Allow to cure for 30 minutes at room temperature.

2. Preheat the oven to 350°F.

3. Place a large cast-iron skillet over medium-high heat. Add the olive oil and, once piping hot, add the salmon fillets, skin side down. Cook until the skin is golden brown, 2 to 3 minutes, then turn the fillets with a large spatula. Place the pan in the oven and cook 3 to 5 minutes, until an instant-read thermometer inserted in the thickest part of a fillet is 122°F for wild, 124°F for farmed, or the fish is cooked to desired doneness. Rest the fillets on a plate, skin side up, for 3 to 4 minutes.

4. Place a fillet in each of four bowls. Top with ginger-garlic chili crisp and serve. If desired, dot the fillets with cilantro, and serve with roasted asparagus and flat-leaf parsley leaves.

GINGER-GARLIC CHILI CRISP

MAKES ABOUT ½ CUP

½ cup vegetable oil

4 medium cloves garlic, minced

¼ cup dried minced white onion

3 tablespoons sesame seeds

2 tablespoons julienned pickled ginger

1 tablespoon dried red Fresno chili, finely crushed

1½ teaspoons kosher salt

1 teaspoon maple sugar or granulated sugar

1. Cook the vegetable oil, garlic, and onion in a small saucepan over medium heat, stirring occasionally, until the garlic and onion are golden brown and the mixture is about 325°F on an instant-read thermometer. Keep an eye on the temperature—you may need to briefly increase the heat to achieve perfect browning.

2. Add the sesame seeds, ginger, chili, salt, and sugar to the oil mixture and stir over medium heat until incorporated. Remove from the heat, allow to cool completely, and pour into a small mason jar or glass container. The chili crisp lasts for 1 week in the refrigerator.

ROASTED SALMON & SOBA NOODLES WITH BROTH

I like to prepare the soba noodles ahead and then reheat them while the salmon is roasting in the oven. The noodles are better when they have time to soak a bit before serving. If you are pressed for time, sear the salmon in a cast-iron skillet for 2 to 3 minutes and then place the fillets in the soba noodle broth to finish cooking. This avoids an extra step, though the salmon will likely break into pieces when you serve it. Either way is fine: The broken salmon will still taste delicious and remain silky smooth.

SERVES 4 ✳ COOK TO 122°F FOR WILD, 124°F FOR FARMED, OR TO DESIRED DONENESS

Four 3-ounce skin-on, boneless salmon fillets

2 tablespoons furikake seasoning

1 tablespoon kosher salt

2 teaspoons freshly ground black pepper

2 tablespoons vegetable oil

1 carrot, peeled and julienned

1 daikon radish, peeled and julienned

4 ounces shiitake mushrooms, stems removed, thinly sliced

One 1-inch piece ginger, peeled, smashed, and minced

2 cups low-sodium chicken broth

½ cup low-sodium tamari

1 pound fresh yakisoba noodles

2 scallions, thinly sliced, for garnish

¼ cup fresh cilantro leaves for garnish

1 nori sheet, julienned, for garnish

1. Season the salmon fillets all over with the furikake, salt, and pepper.

2. Preheat the oven to 400°F.

3. Heat 1 tablespoon of the oil in a large cast-iron skillet over medium-high heat. Place the salmon in the pan skin side down. Cook until the skin starts to crisp and brown, 1 to 2 minutes. Flip and place in the oven. Continue roasting the salmon for 5 to 6 minutes, until an instant-read thermometer inserted in the thickest part of a fillet is 122°F for wild, 124°F for farmed, or the fish is cooked to desired doneness. Rest the fillets on a plate, skin side up, for 3 to 4 minutes.

4. Heat the remaining 1 tablespoon oil in a medium saucepan over medium heat. Add the carrot, radish, mushrooms, and ginger and sauté until the vegetables are just tender, 3 to 4 minutes. Add the chicken broth and tamari and bring to a simmer. Add the noodles and stir. Turn off the heat. Taste and adjust the seasonings with salt and pepper.

5. Place noodles and broth into four bowls and top each with a salmon fillet. Garnish with the scallion, cilantro, and nori.

ROASTED

SALMON & TOASTED COUSCOUS MAC & CHEESE

I love roasted salmon and mac and cheese. This recipe features perfectly roasted salmon atop a bed of creamy couscous mac and cheese. The combination creates a uniquely delicious and nutritious experience that is both comforting and sophisticated. You can replace the couscous with any type of pasta, but the small round texture of the toasted couscous is part of what makes this dish so interesting.

SERVES 4 ✳ COOK TO 122°F FOR WILD, 124°F FOR FARMED, OR TO DESIRED DONENESS

2 teaspoons extra-virgin olive oil, plus more for coating

1 cup Israeli (pearl) couscous

1 tablespoon minced shallots

2 cups low-sodium chicken broth, plus more as needed

½ cup heavy cream

¼ cup diced smoked salmon

½ cup shredded Monterey Jack cheese

¼ cup shredded mild cheddar cheese

Kosher salt and freshly ground black pepper

Four 4-ounce skinless, boneless salmon fillets

1 teaspoon chopped fresh chives for garnish

Flat-leaf parsley leaves for garnish

1 lemon, cut into eight wedges, for garnish

1. Place 1 teaspoon of the olive oil in a medium saucepan over medium heat. Add the couscous and toast until golden brown, 2 to 3 minutes. Add the shallots and stir, cooking for 1 minute more.

2. Add the broth and bring to a simmer. Stir the couscous and continue simmering until the broth is absorbed and the couscous is tender, 6 to 7 minutes. Stir occasionally.

3. Once the couscous is cooked, add the heavy cream and smoked salmon and stir. Remove the pan from the heat. Stir in the cheeses until melted, 2 to 3 minutes. If the mixture is too thick, add more broth until desired texture. Season with salt and pepper.

4. Preheat the oven to 425°F.

5. Place the salmon on a foil-lined baking sheet coated with olive oil and drizzle the fillets with the remaining 1 teaspoon olive oil. Season all over with salt and pepper. Roast the salmon until golden brown, 8 to 10 minutes, and an instant-read thermometer inserted in the thickest part of a fillet is 122°F for wild, 124°F for farmed, or the fish is cooked to desired doneness.

6. Place ½ cup of the couscous into each of four shallow bowls. Top with one salmon fillet. Sprinkle the chives over the top and garnish with parsley and 1 or 2 lemon wedges. Serve at once.

ROASTED SALMON WITH MOREL MUSHROOMS, PEA PUREE & WATERCRESS

Roasted salmon pairs well with any type of mushroom, but fresh morels are one of my favorites. You can find them during spring in high-end food stores and online. Be sure to buy domestic morels—they are best. If too pricey or unavailable, substitute with small brown mushrooms. The creamy sweet pea puree adds richness to the umami flavor of the morels. Watercress adds a peppery bite to the dish. If you don't have watercress, you can use arugula. Cucumber Parisienne are made with a mini-melon baller—you can find one online. The result is a dish worthy of the finest restaurant.

SERVES 4 ✻ COOK TO 122°F FOR WILD, 124°F FOR FARMED, OR TO DESIRED DONENESS

Four 4-ounce skin-on, boneless salmon fillets, preferably center-cut

2 tablespoons extra-virgin olive oil, plus more for coating

1 teaspoon kosher salt, plus more to taste

½ teaspoon freshly ground black pepper, plus more to taste

1 tablespoon unsalted butter

1 cup fresh sweet baby peas or frozen, thawed

¼ cup heavy cream

1 teaspoon rice vinegar

2 ounces fresh morels, cleaned and halved

1 clove garlic, minced

Pinch of fresh thyme leaves

½ English cucumber for garnish (see Note)

1 cup fresh watercress for garnish

½ cup fiddlehead ferns, blanched, for garnish

1. Rub the salmon with 1 tablespoon olive oil, 1 teaspoon salt, and ½ teaspoon pepper, and let rest for 30 minutes.

2. In a medium saucepan, melt the butter over medium heat. Add the peas and cook until bright green, 2 to 3 minutes. Add the heavy cream and bring to a simmer. Simmer for 2 to 3 minutes. Let cool slightly, then transfer the pea mixture to a blender and blend until smooth. Add the vinegar and pulse. Season with salt and pepper.

3. Preheat the oven to 400°F.

4. In a medium bowl, toss the mushrooms with the remaining 1 tablespoon olive oil, garlic, and thyme. Season with salt and pepper. Spread the mushrooms in a single layer on a baking sheet and roast until tender and slightly browned, 5 to 7 minutes. Keep the oven on.

5. Pat the salmon fillets dry with paper towels. Place skin side up on a foil-lined baking sheet coated with oil and roast until the skin is crispy and golden brown, about 7 minutes, and an instant-read thermometer inserted in the thickest part of a fillet is 122°F for wild, 124°F for farmed, or the fish is cooked to desired doneness. Rest the fillets on a plate, skin side up, for 2 to 3 minutes.

6. To assemble, spoon a generous amount of pea puree onto each of four plates. Place a roasted salmon fillet on top of the puree. Arrange the roasted morel mushrooms around the salmon. Garnish with the cucumber, watercress, and fiddlehead ferns, and serve.

Note: To prepare the cucumber Parisienne, use a mini-melon baller, easily found online, to scoop out small balls of cucumber. Avoid the seeds.

ROASTED SALMON WITH TOMATILLO & PEPPER GRATINÉE

Tomatillos and roasted peppers combine to produce a bold flavor that complements sockeye salmon, which was used for this photo. However, you can use this topping for any species of salmon. This recipe is a perfect dish for any special occasion or dinner party.

SERVES 4 ✳ COOK TO 122°F FOR WILD, 124°F FOR FARMED, OR TO DESIRED DONENESS

- **¼ cup plus 3 teaspoons extra-virgin olive oil**
- **One 1½-pound skin-on, boneless side of salmon**
- **1 teaspoon kosher salt, plus more to taste**
- **½ teaspoon granulated sugar**
- **8 fresh, firm medium tomatillos, husked, rinsed, charred, peeled, and quartered (see Note)**
- **1 medium yellow pepper, charred, peeled, and seeded (see Notes, page 87)**
- **1 medium red pepper, charred, peeled, and seeded (see Notes, page 87)**
- **¼ bunch cilantro**
- **3 cloves garlic, coarsely chopped**
- **Juice of 1 lime, plus more to taste**
- **¼ cup kalamata olives, pitted and chopped**
- **½ teaspoon freshly ground black pepper, plus more to taste**
- **½ teaspoon chili powder, cayenne pepper, or Aleppo pepper (optional)**

1. Preheat the oven to 400°F.

2. Line a baking sheet with foil and coat with 1 teaspoon of the olive oil. Pat the salmon dry, place on the baking sheet, and rub with ½ teaspoon salt and the sugar.

3. Reserve 8 to 10 tomatillo quarters in a bowl and put the rest in a food processor with a metal blade. Add the roasted peppers, cilantro, garlic, ¼ cup olive oil, and lime juice and pulse until the mixture combines but is still chunky. Transfer the mixture to a medium bowl and add the olives and ½ teaspoon salt and pepper. Taste and adjust salt, pepper, and lime juice, if needed. Stir in the chili powder, if desired.

4. Spoon half of the tomatillo-pepper mixture over the salmon and place the tomatillo quarters on top. Drizzle with another 2 teaspoons olive oil. Roast until the salmon is slightly golden brown, 8 to 10 minutes, and an instant-read thermometer inserted in the thickest part of a fillet is 122°F for wild, 124°F for farmed, or the fish is cooked to desired doneness. Rest the fish for 3 to 5 minutes before serving.

5. Using the aluminum foil as a sling, transfer the fish to a serving platter. Serve with additional tomatillo mixture on the side.

Note: I like to flame-roast tomatillos and peppers on my stovetop at home. This requires a small stainless-steel baking rack and a strong vent (ours vents to the outside of the house). It can be smoky and a bit messy because of the ash and drippings that fall to the burner. Both are easily cleaned, but this approach may not be possible for some folks. A good alternative is to broil them in a toaster oven until they are charred on the outside. Once charred, let them cool, then peel under cold running water.

ROASTED SALMON WITH ASPARAGUS, SPRING PEAS & POTATOES

This is another spring-inspired recipe. If you prefer to make a one-pan meal, eliminate the peas and simply roast the asparagus with the salmon and potatoes on the same pan. Either way is fine, but I prefer the pea puree and the blanched sweet peas on the side. It adds luxury to the dish.

SERVES 4 ✳ COOK TO 122°F FOR WILD, 124°F FOR FARMED, OR TO DESIRED DONENESS

¼ cup kosher salt, plus more to taste

1 bunch asparagus (16 to 20 stalks), trimmed

1 cup fresh sweet peas

¼ cup rice vinegar

½ cup extra-virgin olive oil, plus more for drizzling

Freshly ground black pepper

Four 4-ounce skin-on, boneless, center-cut salmon loins

1 pound yellow creamer potatoes, peeled and halved

1 bunch opal basil, leaves picked for garnish

1. Preheat the oven to 400°F.

2. Fill a large stockpot with water, add ¼ cup salt, and bring to a boil. Once the water is boiling, prepare an ice-water bath. Add the asparagus and parcook for 3 minutes. Use a slotted spoon to transfer the asparagus to the ice-water bath to stop the cooking process. Transfer to a plate and set aside.

3. Add the peas to the boiling water and parcook for 3 minutes. Strain in a colander set over a sink. Transfer half of the peas to a blender, reserving the other half in a bowl. Add the rice vinegar and blend on high. While blending, drizzle in ¼ cup olive oil and continue to blend until a smooth and creamy sauce has formed. Season to taste with salt and pepper.

4. Place the salmon, skin side down, on a large plate, rub with ¼ cup olive oil, and season with salt and pepper. Let sit at room temperature.

5. In a medium bowl, season the potatoes with salt and pepper, and drizzle with olive oil. Place on a large baking sheet, leaving room in the center for the salmon fillets. Roast until the potatoes just start to brown, about 8 minutes. Remove but keep the oven on.

6. Place the salmon fillets, skin side down, in the center of the baking sheet with the potatoes and return the pan to the oven. Roast for 8 to 10 minutes, until an instant-read thermometer inserted in the thickest part of a fillet is 122°F for wild, 124°F for farmed, or the fish is cooked to desired doneness. If you prefer your asparagus hot, place in a sauté pan over medium heat halfway through cooking the salmon and cook for 4 to 5 minutes to warm through.

7. To serve, place a fillet on each of four plates. Spoon about ¼ cup pea puree next to the salmon. Add a portion of the warm potatoes, peas, and asparagus to each plate. Garnish with the opal basil leaves before serving.

CRISPY ROASTED
SALMON, TOMATOES & HERBS IN SEASONED BROTH

This light, summery dish utilizes salmon bones for a deeply flavored broth that contrasts well with the sweet, acidic flavor of vine-ripened tomatoes. The longer you simmer the bones, the bolder the flavor. If finding fresh salmon bones is too difficult, you can use chicken stock instead. During summer, additional seasonal vegetables, such as broccoli rabe, can be added to the recipe to bring contrast and texture.

SERVES 4 ✳ COOK TO 122°F FOR WILD, 124°F FOR FARMED, OR TO DESIRED DONENESS

Kosher salt

2 tablespoons granulated sugar

Four 3-ounce skin-on, boneless salmon fillets

1 pint cherry tomatoes

1 small bunch fresh basil leaves, stems removed

1 bunch garlic scapes or scallions, cut into ½-inch lengths, tips reserved

¼ cup extra-virgin olive oil, plus more for coating

Freshly ground black pepper

1 pint Salmon Bone Broth (recipe follows), warmed

1. In a small bowl, combine 2 tablespoons salt and the sugar. Place the salmon fillets on a plate and sprinkle the salt-sugar mixture evenly over each piece. Cover loosely with plastic wrap and refrigerate for 1 hour.

2. Bring a large pot of salted water to a boil. When the water comes to a boil, prepare an ice-water bath. Add the tomatoes, basil, and garlic scapes and boil for 20 seconds. Use a slotted spoon to transfer the vegetables and herbs to the ice-water bath. Drain and gently pat dry with paper towels.

3. Preheat the oven to 400°F.

4. Remove the fillets from the refrigerator. Rinse off the salt-sugar mixture under cold running water. Pat dry with paper towels.

5. Place the salmon skin side up on a foil-lined baking sheet coated with olive oil. Brush the tops with ¼ cup olive oil and season with salt and pepper. Roast in the oven for 8 to 10 minutes, until an instant-read thermometer inserted in the thickest part of a fillet is 122°F for wild, 124°F for farmed, or the fish is cooked to desired doneness.

6. To serve, divide the blanched vegetables and herbs among four bowls. Place one salmon fillet in each bowl and pour about ½ cup warm broth over the vegetables to finish.

SALMON BONE BROTH

MAKES 1 PINT

1 pound salmon bones, backbone preferred, cut into 2-inch lengths

Kosher salt and freshly ground black pepper

1 tablespoon extra-virgin olive oil

2 scallions

1 shallot, roughly chopped

1 rib celery, cut into ½-inch lengths

1 medium carrot, peeled and cut into ½-inch lengths

4 sprigs fresh thyme

4 sprigs flat-leaf parsley

1. Preheat the oven to 350°F.

2. Place the salmon bones in a deep roasting pan. Sprinkle with salt and pepper, drizzle with the olive oil, and add the scallions, shallot, celery, and carrot. Roast until the bones are golden brown, 15 minutes.

3. Remove the pan from the oven and drain and reserve any fat and liquid that has collected in the pan; set aside. Add the thyme and parsley to the bones and vegetables in the pan. Add 3 cups water and bring to a simmer over medium-high heat. Simmer for 15 to 20 minutes until flavorful, or longer if a deeper flavor is desired. Strain the broth through a fine-mesh sieve into a medium saucepan. Strain the reserved pan juices through the same sieve and combine with the broth.

4. Place the saucepan over medium-high heat and simmer until reduced to about 2 cups. Taste and season with salt and pepper as needed.

PLANK-ROASTED SALMON WITH CITRUS CILANTRO SALSA

Plank-roasted salmon is delicious and can be prepared outdoors on a grill or indoors in a hot oven, if you have good ventilation. Be sure to soak the cedar planks before use. Serve this dish with your favorite sides, such as potato salad, chilled beets, and pickled purple daikon radish. And be sure to serve a little extra salsa on the side.

SERVES 4 ✳ COOK TO 122°F FOR WILD, 124°F FOR FARMED, OR TO DESIRED DONENESS

¼ cup chopped cilantro stems and leaves

Zest and juice of 1 lime

Zest and juice of 1 lemon

1 tablespoon ground coriander seeds

1 teaspoon kosher salt

½ teaspoon freshly ground black pepper

1 cup fresh, store-bought mild salsa

2 tablespoons extra-virgin olive oil, plus more for coating

One 16-ounce skin-on, boneless salmon fillet

SPECIAL EQUIPMENT

10- to 12-inch-long roasting plank (alder, hickory, or cedar; make sure plank is free of splinters and smooth to the touch)

1. Place a roasting plank in a long, rectangular container and cover with water. Weigh plank down to assure it remains submerged. Soak for 1 hour.

2. In a medium bowl, combine the cilantro, lime and lemon zests and juices, coriander, salt, pepper, and ¾ cup salsa. Refrigerate, covered with plastic wrap, for 30 minutes.

3. Remove the plank from the water and pat dry. Place on a large baking sheet.

4. Preheat the oven to 400°F. Soak a paper towel in olive oil until saturated. Rub the top of the plank with a light coating of olive oil (this will prevent the fish from sticking).

5. Pat the salmon fillet dry. Place the fillet lengthwise on the center of the plank. Rub 2 to 3 tablespoons of the salsa over the fillet. Place the baking sheet with plank and salmon in the oven. Roast for 12 to 15 minutes, until an instant-read thermometer inserted in the thickest part of a fillet is 122°F for wild, 124°F for farmed, or the fish is cooked to desired doneness.

6. Remove from the oven. Once cooled slightly, use oven mitts to transfer the plank to a serving platter. Drizzle the salmon with additional salsa and serve the remaining salsa on the side. (For the photo, and as an alternative, we used a boneless salmon steak wrapped in butcher's twine.)

ACKNOWLEDGMENTS

The Complete Guide to Salmon represents the culmination of extensive research, travel, culinary exploration, and a collaborative effort over several years. Bringing a project of this scope to fruition requires the insight, generosity, and unwavering support of many individuals and organizations. It is with profound gratitude that I acknowledge their essential contributions.

Let me start by offering sincere gratitude to Joe Gurrera for his inspiration and mentorship, and for writing the foreword. Decades ago, Joe set out to be the best fishmonger in the country and achieved just that. It's such an honor to call him a friend.

My exploration of salmon from a culinary perspective was significantly shaped and elevated by the input of two exceptional chefs who are also close friends: Master Chef Robert Mancuso and Michelin-star Chef Marcus Gleadow Ware. Chef Mancuso generously shared his deep culinary wisdom and perspective on preparing salmon during my multiple visits to Seattle and precious time spent in his kitchen in Monterey, California. I recall with particular clarity and appreciation the preparation of a memorable steelhead dish, and his insightful guidance on harnessing the power of fundamental seasonings and the bright acidity of citrus to elevate the natural flavors of the fish. His philosophy and practical knowledge were instrumental in the development and refinement of several recipes featured in this cookbook.

Early in the process, I envisioned undertaking every aspect of the book's production myself—from the narrative and recipes to the photography, prop styling, set design, and food styling. It soon became apparent that this approach was too vast for a single individual, and Chef Ware stepped in as an indispensable collaborator. His expertise in food styling allowed me to concentrate my efforts on the intricate demands of recipe writing, set design, prop selection, and photography. Chef Ware's commitment was extraordinary; it was not uncommon for him to drive from New York City to my studio in Boston, dedicate himself to two demanding twelve-hour workdays, and then make the return journey. He became a vital partner throughout this three-year endeavor, joining me for numerous studio sessions. His collaboration extended to a pivotal trip to Tokyo and Kyoto. This immersion into the culinary landscape of arguably the world's highest per-capita consumers of salmon provided invaluable insights into how salmon is prepared, presented, and revered at its highest levels, directly informing sections of this cookbook focused on global techniques and appreciation. Chef Ware undertook the rigorous testing of the majority of the recipes included here, offering critical feedback and suggesting vital adjustments that ensured their accuracy, reliability, and deliciousness. He worked alongside me in the studio, masterfully food-styling many of the dishes presented in these pages—a monumental task that visually defines the cookbook's culinary content.

Bringing this extensive work into a published form required the expertise and dedication of the team at Rizzoli International Publications. I am deeply grateful to Senior Editor Sandy Gilbert Freidus, whose editorial vision and guidance were fundamental in shaping the narrative and structure of the book. Her experience and discerning eye were essential from conception to completion. The cookbook's aesthetic and layout, so critical for a visually driven guide, are a testament to the talent of designer Jan Derevjanik, who transformed the content into a beautifully coherent and engaging reading experience. Copy-editor Tricia Levi applied meticulous attention to detail, ensuring the accuracy and clarity of the text, which is paramount in a comprehensive reference work. I also wish to extend special thanks to Erin Byers Murray, whose expertise and collaboration in crafting the initial proposal and review of each subsequent revision were absolutely foundational. Her understanding of the publishing landscape and ability to articulate the project's vision were instrumental in securing the interest and eventual acceptance by Rizzoli. Without her critical assistance, this cookbook simply would not have moved forward. It is not lost on me that I ended up with a publishing "dream team." I will be forever grateful.

Visual storytelling through food is central to *The Complete Guide to Salmon*, and my abilities behind the camera have been profoundly influenced by photographer Ron Manville. For nearly twenty years, Ron has served as a mentor, generously sharing his knowledge and demonstrating the principles of light, composition, and technical execution that are essential for compelling photography. His guidance has been foundational to developing the photographic style employed throughout this cookbook, enabling me to capture the beauty and detail of salmon and its preparations in a way that complements the written content. Riding on his coattails gives me great joy.

The comprehensive nature of this guide demanded deep engagement with the salmon industry itself, and I am indebted to several key individuals who opened doors and shared important perspectives. My introduction to the complexities and nuances of farmed salmon came through Peter Gati, founder of Storm Seafood back in the late 1990s. His initial insights sparked a deeper investigation into this critical sector of the industry. Ricardo Garcia, CEO of Camanchaca S.A. in Santiago, Chile, provided important and more recent perspectives from a leading producer. I am deeply grateful to Dr. Rolando Ibarra, senior fellow in aquaculture and sustainability at the Monterey Bay Aquarium. Over the past eight years, Rolando has shared invaluable scientific insights into salmon as a biological category, particularly concerning aquaculture practices and sustainability challenges. My most sincere and profound thanks, however, are reserved for Arturo Clement. As one of the true pioneers and grandfathers of the salmon industry in Chile, Arturo provided unprecedented access and shared information with a level of transparency I could never have anticipated. His depth of understanding was pivotal in gaining a full view of the history the Chilean salmon industry and current state of salmon globally. There are many, many more people to thank—to the rest, please accept my sincere gratitude.

Finally, and most importantly, I extend my heartfelt thanks to my wonderful family. Undertaking a project of this magnitude over nearly three years inevitably requires sacrifice and immense patience from those closest to you. My family allowed me the necessary space and time to immerse myself fully in the demanding process of research, writing, and production. They navigated the disruptions to our household with grace, taking in stride the numerous research trips to far-flung places like Japan, Chile, and Alaska and the fifteen-hour photo shoots that commandeered our kitchen and dining room for weeks on end. Among these disruptions they radiated the same quiet support and encouragement they have always offered when I take on a new project or endeavor. The book is as much a product of their love as it is of my own efforts. I have the best family a man could ask for. The depth of my gratitude is immeasurable.

Atlantic salmon being commercially processed for export to the United States.

INDEX

JAMES E. GRIFFIN is an internationally known food and culinary expert and consultant, as well as a professor at Johnson & Wales University. Griffin has served as the owner and manager of multiple food-related businesses. He has appeared on national and local broadcast media, and has presented many seminars and written articles on seafood sustainability and the hospitality and food service industry.

Dr. Griffin earned a BS in food service management and an MS in hospitality administration at Johnson & Wales, and an EdD from Boston University. He has a Management and Leadership in Higher Education certificate from the Harvard Graduate School of Education, and an Executive Certificate in Strategy and Innovation from the Sloan School of Management at the Massachusetts Institute of Technology. Early in his career, he won multiple gold medals as a member of the 1992 US Culinary Olympic Team, competing in US and international events including Hotelympia in London in 1991 and the Culinary Olympics in Frankfurt, Germany, in 1992. He was born and raised in Gloucester, Massachusetts, the oldest fishing port in the US, as part of a family with centuries-old ties to the maritime industry in New England.

MARCUS GLEADOW WARE was born in London and wanted to pursue a culinary career from the time he was a teen. After taking a job as a dishwasher at a gastropub in Islington, he fell in love with the unique vibe of the restaurant's kitchen. In 1995, his passion for cooking earned him a traineeship at the world-renowned Savoy Hotel that included studying at the Académie Culinaire de France. During this time, he received the Eurest prize for "best young chef of the year." Subsequently, Chef Ware worked in some of London's finest kitchens, including Cliveden House and Marco Pierre White's L'Escargot. In 2007, he worked as a senior sous-chef at Aureole. Three years later, restaurateur/owner Chef Charlie Palmer promoted him to executive chef. Today, he is a highly sought-after corporate and consulting chef who helped to open Nantucket's Greydon House and the RH Guesthouse New York. *The Complete Guide to Salmon* is Chef Ware's first formal foray into food styling.

JOE GURRERA is the owner of Citarella, a group of popular epicurean markets, which got its start as one of the original and most-respected neighborhood seafood shops in New York. He grew up in the fish business, learning firsthand the subtle differences between the flavors and textures of dozens of varieties of seafood. Gurrera also owns Lockwood & Winant, a wholesale seafood company at the iconic Fulton Fish Market, and the hospitality seafood purveyor Citarella Purveying, which supplies some of the most prestigious restaurants in the United States. Gurrera is an industry leader, selling several million pounds of seafood a year.

James Griffin outside the Tsukiji Outer Market in Tokyo, November 2024.

The net pens of a salmon hatchery in Lake Llanquihue, in Puerto Varas, Los Lagos, Chile.

BACK COVER: The ferry terminal in Kingston, Washington, as seen from Puget Sound.

Illustration Credits Pages 19, 20, 21, 22, 23, 33 (center): copyright © via Getty Images, from the following collections: pages 19, 21, 22, 23 Chum Salmon, Coho Salmon, Pink Salmon, and Sockeye Salmon credit: Dorling Kindersley/Dorling Kindersley RF; pages 20, 22, 33 King Salmon credit: George Peters/E+; pages 22, 23 Artic Char credit: Elmar Krenkel/image BROKER; pages 22, 23 Atlantic Salmon and Steelhead Salmon credit: MIXA Co. Ltd./ MIXA; Page 33: Fishing industry seafood production, ocean commercial fishermen working (fishing and selling products), copyright © Freepik, sponsored by Shutterstock, Getty Images; Life cycle of salmon infographics, copyright © Macrovector/Dreamstime.com; Getty Images; End User Consumer, iStock, credit: Lyubov Ovsyannikova, Getty Images

First published in the
United States of America in 2026 by
Rizzoli International Publications, Inc.
49 West 27th Street
New York, NY 10001
www.rizzoliusa.com

Publisher: Charles Miers
Editor: Sandra Gilbert Freidus
Design: Jan Derevjanik
Production Manager: Rebecca Ambrose
Editorial Coordination:
Tricia Levi and Candice Fehrman
Editorial Consultant: Erin Byers Murray
Index: Cathy Dorsey
Food Stylist: Marcus Gleadow Ware
Managing Editor: Lynn Scrabis

ISBN: 978-0-8478-7648-8
Library of Congress Control Number: 2025943029

Printed in China
2026 2027 2028 2029 / 10 9 8 7 6 5 4 3 2 1

The authorized representative in the EU for product safety and compliance is
Mondadori Libri S.p.A., via Gian Battista Vico 42,
Milan, Italy, 20123,
www.mondadori.it

Visit us online:
Instagram: @RizzoliBooks
Facebook.com/RizzoliNewYork
Youtube.com/user/RizzoliNY